STUDY GUIDE

Western Civilizations

Fifteenth Edition

VOLUME 1

Western Civilizations

Volume 1

FIFTEENTH EDITION

Margaret Minor

NICHOLLS STATE UNIVERSITY

Paul Wilson

NICHOLLS STATE UNIVERSITY

W • W • NORTON & COMPANY • NEW YORK • LONDON

Copyright © 2005 by W. W. Norton & Company, Inc.

ISBN 0-393-92583-8 (pbk)

W. W. Norton & Company, Inc., 500 Fifth Avenue, New York, N. Y. 10110
    www.wwnorton.com
W. W. Norton & Company Ltd., Castle House, 75/76 Wells Street, London W1T 3QT

1 2 3 4 5 6 7 8 9 0

CONTENTS

PREFACE

This *Study Guide* is designed to complement *Western Civilizations*, Fifteenth Edition, by Coffin, Lerner, Meacham, and Stacey. It is specifically addressed to students as a user-friendly manual that will enable them to grasp the significance of the material covered in each chapter. Instructors will find it beneficial to assign the *Study Guide* to improve student comprehension and to use certain parts of it for tests, quizzes, class discussions, and research assignments. The *Study Guide* provides a step-by-step approach to each chapter in *Western Civilizations*. We have designed exercises to promote understanding of specific facts and ideas and to promote critical thinking and analytical skills. Students who complete all the exercises will have a thorough grasp of the material covered in the text.

Through over twenty years of college teaching, we have worked with a variety of students who have provided insight into this *Study Guide*. Most students enrolled in a Western civilizations course are entering freshmen who need guidance in how to prepare for such a college course. In many instances, classes are so large that instructors cannot give the guidance they would like to provide. Sometimes, students are working and do not have time to meet with instructors. Some students just prefer to work on their own. These are among the factors that have contributed to our preparation of this guide, which we know will be helpful.

Each chapter of the *Study Guide* begins with an overview of the material covered in the chapter followed by an outline. Each chapter contains identification terms, multiple-choice questions, matching items, true/false questions, chronological order exercises, and short-answer and discussion questions. Identification terms allow students to address specific items and examine their significance. In defining identification terms, a student should be able to explain carefully and fully the importance of a person, event, or term. The multiple choice and matching items and true/false questions test students' ability to remember certain facts, events, individuals, trends, and explanations in the text as well as their critical reasoning skills. Chronological order exercises enable students to arrange events often included thematically within the text in correct sequence.

The exercises are designed as building blocks to complement the short-answer and essay questions which show how events, facts, and ideas fit into a proper interpretation of history. Questions break down material into smaller components and reveal how ideas and events are interconnected. They provide an excellent opportunity to analyze information, and students should fully explain answers by giving detailed responses with examples. Short-answer questions are grouped together thematically to provide ideas for longer essays. Some questions specifically address document readings included in the text.

CHAPTER 1 | The Origins of Western Civilizations

This chapter focuses on how civilization came about. What you want to understand are the steps in that development. The chapter traces the development in both Mesopotamia and Egypt. Think about what civilization is and then compare the development in both these areas.

CHAPTER OUTLINE

1. Introduction

2. The Stone Age background
   a. Upper Paleolithic era
   b. The Neolithic Revolution
      i. The origins of food production in the ancient Near East
      ii. The great villages of the Near East

3. The development of civilization in Mesopotamia
   a. Ubaid culture
   b. Urbanism in the Uruk Period (4300–2900 B.C.E.)
   c. The development of writing

4. The Sumerians Enter History
   a. The Early Dynastic Period begins (2900–2500 B.C.E.)
   b. Sumerian religion
   c. Science, technology, and trade
   d. The end of the Early Dynastic Period
   e. The Akkadian empire (2350–2160 B.C.E.)
   f. The dynasty of Ur (2100–2000 B.C.E.)
   g. The "Sumerian Renaissance" and the rise of the Amorites
   h. The Old Babylonian empire
      i. Religion and law
      ii. Old Babylonian society
      iii. Hammurabi's legacy

5. Development of civilization in Egypt
   a. Predynastic Egypt (c. 10,000–3100 B.C.E.)
   b. The unification of Egypt: the Archaic Period (3100–2686 B.C.E.)
   c. Language and writing
   d. The Old Kingdom (2686–2125 B.C.E.)
      i. Imhotep and the "Step Pyramid"
      ii. Society in Old Kingdom Egypt
      iii. Women in the Old Kingdom
      iv. Science and technology
      v. Egyptian religion and world view
         1. The Egyptian death cult
      vi. The end of the Old Kingdom
   e. Middle Kingdom Egypt (2055–1650 B.C.E.)

6. Conclusion

IDENTIFY

1. civilization
2. Mesopotamia
3. Paleolithic era
4. Neolithic era
5. Jericho
6. Ubaid culture
7. Uruk
8. cuneiform
9. Sumerians
10. *Epic of Gilgamesh*
11. *lugal*
12. Sargon

13. Hammurabi
14. Old Kingdom
15. Middle Kingdom
16. hieroglyphs
17. Rosetta Stone
18. Imhotep
19. Djoser
20. Osiris

MULTIPLE CHOICE

1. The Paleolithic Age is characterized by
   a. the production of subsistence agriculture and urban communities.
   b. a rigid division of labor between upper and lower classes.
   c. the existence of small, hunter-gatherer societies.
   d. the complete absence of art and technology.

2. Which of the following best describes a Neolithic community?
   a. a village that regularly moves to remain near migrating herds
   b. a settled community based on farming
   c. a community in which power is shared by the wealthiest citizens
   d. a settlement that has a sophisticated, written language

3. The earliest evidence of a community with domesticated cattle herds is _____.
   a. Jericho
   b. Sumer
   c. Çatal Hüyük
   d. Uruk

4. Civilization began in Mesopotamia because
   a. the first cities emerged there.
   b. the first written language developed there.
   c. the region contained the first permanent settlements.
   d. of the importance of religion in the region.

5. The basic political unit in Sumer was the _____.
   a. village
   b. city–state
   c. empire
   d. kingdom

6. Mesopotamian religion featured
   a. benevolent gods and a pleasant afterlife.
   b. a rigid monotheism with explicit commandments and elaborate rituals.
   c. cruel, impetuous, and vindictive gods who needed to be appeased.
   d. none of the above.

7. Sumerian achievements include all of the following except
   a. the solar calendar.
   b. sophisticated measuring and surveying techniques.
   c. the first great work of literature.
   d. a written language.

8. Semitic peoples are related by _____.
   a. religion
   b. blood
   c. ethnicity
   d. language

9. Hammurabi
   a. cleverly used diplomacy to consolidate his rule.
   b. defeated Sargon to create a new Akkadian empire.
   c. is generally credited as the author of the *Epic of Gilgamesh*.
   d. died in battle against the Amorites.

10. Which of the following is true concerning Predynastic Egypt?
    a. The remarkably abundant archeological evidence provides the names of the first pharaohs.
    b. It was populated by peoples from North Africa, East Africa, and western Asia.
    c. Its cities were much larger than those in Sumer.
    d. Pyramid construction symbolized its wealth and power.

11. Egyptians believed pharaohs to be
    a. divine.
    b. only human but favored by the gods.
    c. less important than priests.
    d. the earthly manifestation of Osiris.

12. The Old Kingdom in Egypt
    a. saw the political and cultural unification of Upper and Lower Egypt under the rule of King Scorpion.
    b. was the time when the pyramids of Giza were constructed.
    c. collapsed under the assault of the Akkadians.
    d. was largely decentralized with power shared by pharaohs and local governors.

13. Egyptian women
    a. regularly held positions in state government.
    b. had the same legal rights as men.
    c. could not defend themselves in court.
    d. had a surprising degree of legal rights for their time.

14. Egyptian religion
    a. was the most influential of the ancient world.
    b. only allowed pharaohs to gain immortality.
    c. was polytheistic and offered the opportunity for a pleasant afterlife.
    d. was characterized by its pessimism.

15 The Egyptian Middle Kingdom
   a. was centered around its new capital at Memphis.
   b. witnessed the strengthening of the power of pharaohs.
   c. saw Egypt take a greater interest in lands beyond its borders.
   d. all of the above.

MATCHING

1. Mesopotamia
2. Uruk
3. ziggurat
4. cuneiform
5. lugal
6. Gilgamesh
7. Sargon
8. hieroglyphs
9. Champollion
10. Imhotep
11. Osiris
12. *Duat*
13. *ma'at*
14. Nitocris
15. Ra

a. sacred carvings
b. script developed by the Sumerians
c. judge of the deceased's *ka*
d. king of Uruk who unsuccessfully sought to gain immortality
e. a temple for the gods
f. land between the rivers
g. female pharaoh
h. Egyptian concept of harmony, order, justice, and truth
i. designed the Step Pyramid
j. led his city's army in battle
k. Egyptian sun god
l. developed from a Neolithic village into a Sumerian city
m. first conqueror of Sumer
n. deciphered the Rosetta Stone
o. the land of death

TRUE/FALSE

1. The Sumerians developed a lunar calendar consisting of twelve months.

2. The first Sumerian *lugal* to create a genuine empire was Naram–Sin.

3. The Sumerians and Akkadians were culturally similar.

4. Under Hammurabi's code, women had no right to divorce abusive husbands because wives were regarded as property.

5. During the Old Kingdom, the Pharaoh Imhotep elevated the worship of Osiris.

6. Papyrus was essential for the Mesopotamians to maintain accurate records.

7. The first Egyptian cities emerged in Upper Egypt.

8. In comparison to other women in the ancient world, Egyptian women had greater legal status.

9. Osiris and Seth were twin gods of mummification.

10. The Egyptians held a more positive view of the gods than the Mesopotamians did.

PUT THE FOLLOWING ITEMS IN CHRONOLOGICAL ORDER

1. Construction of the Great Pyramid of Giza _____

2. Rule of Hammurabi _____

3. Development of cuneiform _____

4. Conquest of Sumer by Sargon _____

5. Founding of Jericho _____

6. Discovery of the Rosetta Stone _____

7. The Uruk period _____

SHORT ANSWER AND ESSAY QUESTIONS

I. Mesopotamia

A. Early stages of development
   1. What are the characteristics of civilization?
   2. What are the characteristics of the two stages of the Stone Age?
   3. What are the basic patterns of urban life? How did these patterns emerge?
   4. During the Neolithic stage how did the climate change? How did this affect what was going on? How did this lead to a revolution in human history?
   5. Why was it possible to have permanent and semi-permanent settlements?
   6. Explain why storage was such a crucial intermediary step to settlements. Describe the elements involved and the effects on human social relations.

B. Social and economic developments
   1. What were the reasons given for religious speculation? How did this affect social organization?
   2. Explain the importance of trade in the social and economic world.
   3. What was traded? How did this affect the organization of society?
   4. What were the principle influences behind the early emergence of urban life in Mesopotamia?

5. In the development of the Ubaid culture, what were the most consistent features? Show how these features made the civilization more complex by listing the organizational ways that the society worked.

6. Consider the developments of this period by showing why they were important to the society and how they are important to people today.

C. Development of religion and government
   1. Why did a common religion not create peace among the Sumerians?
   2. What elements were shared by various centers of Sumerian culture?
   3. What was the form of government used by the Sumerians? Did it work?
   4. What were the reasons for conflict among the Sumerians in the Early Dynastic Period?
   5. What parts of the *Epic of Gilgamesh* portray society?
   6. Explain the role of religion in society and consider Sumerian attitudes toward the gods and their view of the afterlife.
   7. Compare the descriptions in *The Flood: Two Accounts* and tell how they are similar.
   8. Show the chronology of the contributions of Sumerians by listing what they contributed and when. What does this demonstrate about how one thing leads to another?

D. New approaches
   1. How did the view of the afterlife change during the Early Dynastic Period?
   2. What was the political change during the Early Dynastic Period?
   3. Where did the Akkadians come from? What other groups were part of this language group?
   4. How did the Akkadians and the Sumerians differ?
   5. How did Hammurabi build his empire? How did the view of the god Marduk relate to society? How did Hammurabi use laws to bind the empire?
   6. Read the document *The Code of Hammurabi*. Do any of the laws in *The Code of Hammurabi* seem familiar? Why? Which of the laws surprises you? What characteristics of the code do you think are different from our laws?
   7. What were the divisions within the Amorite-Babylonian society?

II. Egypt

A. List the following periods in Ancient Egypt in chronological order and give the date of each.
   Middle Kingdom
   Archaic Period
   Second Intermediate Period
   The Old Kingdom
   Predynastic Egypt
   First Intermediate Period

B. Egyptian development of civilization
   1. In what ways did patterns of development in early Egypt differ from those in Sumer?
   2. How did geography and the environment contribute to the development of civilization in early Egypt?
   3. When and where were the first Egyptian cities founded? Why were they established in these places?

C. Egyptian religion and government
   1. What was the role of religious centers in Egypt?
   2. What are the basic features of the pharaohs' rule?
   3. How were the government and religion linked in Archaic Egypt?
   4. What do *The Egyptian Book of the Dead* and *The Instruction of Ptah-Hotep* tell us about the expectations of Egyptian society?
   5. Explain the Egyptians' belief in the "cyclical nature in the universe." How was this idea of "cyclical nature in the universe" expressed in their religion?
   6. What were the various social groups in the Egyptian Old Kingdom?
   7. What was unique about the Old Kingdom for women?
   8. What were the advances the Egyptians made in the calculation of time?
   9. The mythology of the *Osiris* story is important in understanding Egypt. How is this connected to the geography of Egypt? How is this connected to the death cult?
   10. List four of the Egyptian gods and describe their jobs or roles in nature.
   11. What were the changes between the Old Kingdom and the Middle Kingdom in Egypt?

D. Egyptian economics
   1. What was the connection between power, expansion, and trade?
   2. How did Egyptian expansion relate to the Egyptians' view of the world?
   3. How did the position of the pharaoh change between the Old Kingdom and the Middle Kingdom?

E. Write an essay that describes the development of civilization. Compare and contrast the Egyptian and Mesopotamian civilizations.

MULTIPLE CHOICE KEY

1. c
2. b
3. c
4. a
5. b
6. c
7. a
8. d
9. a
10. b
11. a
12. b
13. d
14. c
15. c

CHRONOLOGICAL ORDER KEY

5, 7, 3, 1, 4, 2, 6

MATCHING KEY

1. f
2. l
3. e
4. b
5. j
6. d
7. m
8. a
9. n
10. i
11. c
12. o
13. h
14. g
15. k

TRUE/FALSE KEY

1. T
2. F
3. T
4. F
5. F
6. F
7. F
8. T
9. F
10. T

CHAPTER 2

Gods and Empires in the Ancient Near East, 1700–500 B.C.E

There are two main themes for this chapter. One shows the growth of empires in the Late Bronze Age and their connection via international trade. These empires were more unified than earlier ones. Another theme is the development of religious beliefs and specific theological doctrines. Religion and politics were bound together during this period because the rulers often saw themselves as "chosen instruments of their god's divine will".

CHAPTER OUTLINE

1. Introduction

2. The Indo-European migrations
   a. The rise of Anatolia
   b. Hittites and Kassites
   c. The kingdom of the Mitanni

3. Egypt in the second millennium B.C.E.
   a. The New Kingdom (1550–1075 B.C.E.)
      i. Pharaonic rule in Dynasty 18
      ii. Queen Hatshepsut and Thutmosis III
      iii. Religious change and religious challenge
         1. The temple of Amon
         2. The reign of Akhenaten (1352–1336 B.C.E.)

4. The International System of the Late Bronze Age
   a. International diplomacy
   b. International trade
   c. Expansion and fragility

5. Aegean civilization: Minoans and Mycenaeans
   a. The Minoan sea empire
   b. The Mycenaeans
   c. The sea peoples and the end of the Bronze Age

6. The small-scale states of the Early Iron Age
   a. The Phoenicians
      i. Phoenician cities
      ii. Cultural influence
   b. The Philistines
   c. The Hebrews
      i. Origins
      ii. Hebrews and Philistines
      iii. Consolidation of the Hebrew kingdom
      iv. The reign of King Solomon (973–937 B.C.E)
      v. The northern and southern kingdoms
   d. The Assyrian empire
      i. The Middle Assyrian Period (1362–859 B.C.E.)
      ii. The neo-Assyrian empire (859–627 B.C.E.)
         1. Government and administration
         2. The Assyrian military-religious ethos
      iii. The end of Assyria and its legacy
   e. The Persians
      i. The origins of the Persian empire
      ii. The consolidation of the Persian empire
      iii. Zoroastrianism
   f. The development of Hebrew monotheism
      i. From monolatry to monotheism
      ii. Judaism takes shape

6. Conclusion

IDENTIFY

1. Sir William Jones
2. Anatolia
3. Assyrians
4. Cappadocia
5. Hittites
6. Kassites
7. Mitanni
8. New Kingdom
9. Hatshepsut
10. Temple of Amon
11. Amenhotep IV
12. Heinrich Schliemann

13. The Minoans
14. The Mycenaeans
15. The Phoenicians
16. The Philistines
17. The Hebrews
18. David
19. Solomon
20. Amos

MULTIPLE CHOICE

1. Indo-European languages include all of the following except _____.
   a. Sanskrit
   b. Greek
   c. Hebrew
   d. Latin

2. The founder of the Hittite Kingdom was _____.
   a. Hattusilis
   b. Mursilis I
   c. Shalmaneser I
   d. Tiglath-Pileser

3. The Hyksos
   a. destroyed the kingdom of the Mitanni and subjugated the Assyrians.
   b. were the first foreign invaders to conquer Egypt.
   c. invented the light, horse-drawn chariot with spoked wheels.
   d. introduced monotheism to Egypt.

4. The Egyptian New Kingdom witnessed
   a. the creation of a more democratic government.
   b. the triumph of monotheism.
   c. the rise of warrior pharaohs and an Egyptian empire.
   d. all of the above.

5. Akhenaten attempted to
   a. concentrate exlusively on military affairs to strengthen Egypt's position in the Near East.
   b. increase the power of the priesthood of Amon at Thebes.
   c. direct Egyptian religion toward monotheism.
   d. rule jointly with his sister, Hatshepsut.

6. Which of the following is not correct concerning the Late Bronze Age?
   a. a balance of power emerged among the great powers.
   b. diplomacy largely removed warfare as an aspect of international relations.
   c. trade developed as an important part of international relations.
   d. the economies of different eastern Mediterranean states became more integrated.

7. The collapse of the Hittite and Egyptian empires
   a. created a power vacuum that allowed new, small states to emerge.
   b. allowed the Sea Peoples to control Greece.
   c. had little effect on the international system of the Late Bronze Age.
   d. none of the above.

8. The most important contribution the Phoenicians made to Western civilization was their _____.
   a. religion
   b. legal system
   c. alphabet
   d. military innovations

9. King Solomon's reign was marked by
   a. a strengthening of Hebrew tribal leadership.
   b. final defeat of the Philistines at the Battle of Megiddo.
   c. its simplicity and democracy-like constitutional reforms.
   d. ruthless and despotic rule featuring high taxes and forced labor.

10. The Assyrian military included which of the following formations?
    a. heavily armored shock troops
    b. combat engineers for siege warfare
    c. an armored cavalry force
    d. all of the above

11. The Assyrian empire's greatest legacy was
    a. its collection of Mesopotamian literature from the library in Nineveh.
    b. the farsightedness of its political rule that served as a model for the Greeks and Romans.
    c. its remarkable appreciation and tolerance for its conquered subjects.
    d. its religion which influenced the development of Judaism.

12. The Persians
    a. were far more brutal in governing their empire than the Assyrians.
    b. generally tolerated and respected cultures they controlled.
    c. created an empire almost as large as the former Hittite empire.
    d. allied with the Greeks to defeat the Chaldeans.

13. Zoroastrianism
    a. was a purely monotheistic religion only practiced by Persian emperors.
    b. pointed to a final day of judgment when good would triumph over evil.
    c. denied the possibility of free will because humans were completely manipulated by Ahriman.

d. was a religion whose ethical teachings were borrowed entirely from Judaism.

14. Which of the following is not true concerning the Hebrews?
    a. They were always monotheists who remained faithful to Yahweh, with a few exceptions, throughout their history.
    b. Their teachings promoted universal ethical principles.
    c. Their prophets called upon all Hebrews to worship Yahweh exclusively.
    d. They split into two kingdoms following the death of Solomon.

15. The Babylonian Captivity specifically refers to the period
    a. immediately following the destruction of Israel by the Assyrians.
    b. when the Hebrews neglected Yahweh and began recognizing other gods.
    c. when the Persian emperor Darius forced the Hebrews to convert to Zoroastrianism.
    d. from the conquest of Judah until the Persian victory over the Chaldeans.

MATCHING

1. Hatshepsut
2. Ahmose
3. Valley of the Kings
4. Aten
5. Schliemann
6. Minoans
7. Sea Peoples
8. Saul
9. David
10. Sargon II
11. Cyrus
12. Assur
13. Nineveh
14. Marathon
15. Ahura-Mazda

a. destroyed the kingdom of Israel
b. god promoted by Akhenaten
c. Greek sea-empire
d. site of major Greek victory over the Persians
e. a female pharaoh
f. ended the Babylonian Captivity
g. expelled the Hyksos from Egypt
h. Persian god of light, truth, and righteousness
i. first king of the Hebrews
j. Assyrian capital
k. discovered the site of Troy
l. Established the Hebrew capital at Jerusalem
m. chief Assyrian god
n. credited with destroying the Egyptian and Hittite empires
o. burial site for New Kingdom pharaohs

TRUE/FALSE

1. Trade, diplomacy, and internationalism increased during the Late Bronze Age.
2. Because of their close relationship with the Egyptians, the Hittites adopted hieroglyphics to write their own language.
3. The Kingdom of the Mitanni included the upper Euphrates and northern Syria.
4. Thutmosis III took Megiddo from the kingdom of Kadesh.
5. The priests of Amon at Thebes concentrated only on religious affairs and refrained from involvement in political matters.
6. The pharaoh Tutankhamen continued to promote the worship of Aten but his successors restored the god Amon and his priesthood.
7. Little is known about Minoan civilization because the Minoans possessed no written language.
8. After Solomon died, the Hebrew kingdom split into two kingdoms.
9. Tolerance and benevolence characterized Assyrian attitudes toward their conquered peoples.
10. Zorastrianism shares few similarities with Judaism and Christianity.

PUT THE FOLLOWING ITEMS IN CHRONOLOGICAL ORDER

1. The Babylonian Captivity _____
2. The reign of Akhenaten _____
3. The collapse of the Hittites _____
4. The Battle of Marathon _____
5. The reign of King Solomon _____
6. The reign of Sennacherib _____
7. The destruction of the northern Hebrew Kingdom of Israel _____
8. The beginning of the Egyptian New Kingdom _____

SHORT ANSWER AND ESSAY QUESTIONS

A. Short Answer Questions

1. Give the chronology of the kingdoms in Mesopotamia and the contributions or innovations of each.

2. List the important pharaohs of the New Kingdom and the dates of their reigns.

3. What were the results of the Egyptian campaign against the Mitanni?

4. List the various products of each state involved in international trade.

5. List the results of the Sea Peoples' destruction.

6. Trace the development of the Hebrews into a kingdom.
   a. What were the stages in this development?
   b. How did this development continue?
   c. Why did it break apart?

7. List the rulers of the Assyrian empire and their dates.

8. Trace the victories of Cyrus by listing them along with their dates. Look at a map to see the locations of these while you trace them.

B. Ancient Empires

1. How did the trade networks with the Assyrians contribute to growth in the areas of Anatolia, northern Syria and Mesopotamia? How did trade contribute to other developments in this region?

2. What was the importance of the Hittites? How did they differ from earlier groups in Mesopotamia?

3. In the "Tawagalawas Letter" what does king Hattusilis want from his counterpart?

4. Consider the importance of language. How is it used as a means of defining a population? Give examples. What are the languages we find reference to in this chapter?

5. Explain what was "New" in the New Kingdom of Egypt compared to the Old and Middle Kingdoms.

6. What was the importance of the Hyksos in the Egyptian view of themselves?

7. What were the changes to the social structure in the Egyptian New Kingdom? How did these new classes come about?

8. Give three of the international characteristics of the powerful states during the millennium.

9. The first European cultures we encounter are the Mycenaean and the Minoan. What are the characteristics of each? How are they similar?

10. Consider the use of the Bible as an historical source. What do its characteristics tell us about sources in general?

11. What were the reasons for Assyrian power? Make sure you consider the organization of the administration of the state and the military aspects of its power.

12. How does the inscription of the Senjirli Stele of King Esarhaddon demonstrate the "bombastic propaganda" of Assyrian kingship?

13. How did the Persian empire differ from earlier states in the region? Why do you think these differences came about? Again, as you did with Assyrian power, consider the administration of the state along with the military aspects.

C. Egyptian and Near Eastern Religions

1. In the Egyptian New Kingdom, why did the priests of Amon-Ra get more political clout than the military?

2. A new form of religion developed in the Egyptian New Kingdom under Amenhotep IV. What were the central changes in this new view of religion?

3. Compare and contrast the *Hymn to Aten* and *Psalm 104.*

4. Show how the understanding of religion by the Hebrews parallels their political development. You can begin the process by listing the changing characteristics of Yahweh at different times. How did their religion contribute to their identity?

5. What were the characteristics of Zoroastrianism? How did this religion influence Persian rule?

6. What were the major contributions of the Hebrew religion?

7. What are the differences between the two descriptions of Saul's anointing?

8. How did religion shape the government in the following states: Egypt, the neo-Assyrian empire, Hebrew, and Persia?

MULTIPLE CHOICE KEY

1. c
2. a
3. b
4. c
5. c
6. b
7. a
8. c
9. d
10. d
11. a
12. b
13. b
14. a
15. d

TRUE/FALSE KEY

1. T
2. F
3. T
4. T
5. F
6. F
7. F
8. T
9. F
10. F

CHRONOLOGICAL ORDER KEY

8, 2, 3, 5, 7, 6, 1, 4

MATCHING KEY

1. e
2. g
3. o
4. b
5. k
6. c
7. n
8. i
9. l
10. a
11. f
12. m
13. j
14. d
15. h

CHAPTER 3 | The Greek Experiment

This chapter examines the development of civilization in Greece. As you explore the ideas of the Greek experiment, consider how the values and the system of beliefs were a departure from what had been the normal approach until then. These values were connected to both the view of politics and the view of humanity. One of the major components is the ideal of the nature of humans and the Western concept of "humanity" and of individuals. Another theme throughout this chapter is the development of a "political" awareness.

CHAPTER OUTLINE

1. Introduction

2. The Dark Age of Greece (1150–800 B.C.E.)
   a. Homer and the heroic tradition
   b. Foreign contacts and the rise of the polis

3. Archaic Greece (800–480 B.C.E.)
   a. Colonization and Panhellenism
   b. Hoplite warfare
   c. Aristocratic culture and the rise of tyranny
   d. Lyric poetry

4. The Archaic Polis in Action
   a. Athens
   b. Sparta
   c. Miletus

5. The Persian wars
   a. The Ionian Revolt (499–494 B.C.E.)
   b. Marathon and its aftermath
   c. Xerxes' invasion

6. The Golden Age of classical Greece
   a. Periclean Athens
   b. Literature and drama
   c. Art and architecture
   d. Women and men in the daily life of Athens

7. League building and the Peloponnesian War
   a. The Peloponnesian War erupts
   b. The end of the war
   8. Greek thought
   a. The Pythagoreans and the Sophists
   b. The life and thought of Socrates

9. Conclusion

IDENTIFY

1. Dark Age
2. Homer
3. polis
4. hoplite
5. tyrant
6. Xerxes
7. Athens
8. Solon
9. Cleisthenes
10. Sparta
11. Helots
12. Miletus
13. Persian wars
14. Delian League
15. Pericles
16. Marathon
17. Thucydides
18. Peloponnesian War
19. Pythagoreans
20. Socrates

MULTIPLE CHOICE

1. The Dark Age of Greece was a period of
   a. population growth.
   b. construction of citadels to fend off the Dorians.
   c. massive depopulation.
   d. war between the Greeks and the Persians.

2. The basic political unit of ancient Greece was the
   a. empire.
   b. league.
   c. kingdom.
   d. polis.

3. In Archaic Greece, aristocratic military dominance ended with
   a. the conquest of much of southern Italy.
   b. the use of hoplite tactics.
   c. the Dorian invasion.
   d. increased contact between Greeks and Phoenicians.

4. Greek tyrants
   a. frequently consolidated aristocratic authority within the poleis.
   b. often extended political rights to the people, the *demos*.
   c. were universally despised by all groups of Greeks.
   d. destroyed democratic movements among hoplites.

5. The Greeks regarded homosexuality as
   a. a sin and a sin of faithlessness.
   b. largely a normal practice.
   c. an acceptable activity if devoid of intimacy.
   d. none of the above.

6. Lyric poets
   a. continued the tradition of Homer by writing epics only about warriors seeking honor.
   b. became increasingly involved in the political affairs of Athens.
   c. often wrote about themselves, their feelings, and their own interests.
   d. wrote mostly about the gods and their adventures on Mount Olympus.

7. Solon's reforms included all of the following except
   a. limiting debt slavery to no more than two years.
   b. promotion of grape and olive cultivation.
   c. broadening political participation.
   d. establishing a more equitable court system.

8. To preserve Athenian democracy, Cleisthenes introduced the practice of ostracism which
   a. limited the number of consecutive years archons could serve.
   b. made it illegal for a tyrant to govern.
   c. banished from Athens for ten years individuals considered politically dangerous.
   d. gave each Athenian hoplite a vote on the council.

9. All of the following are true of Sparta except
   a. Spartan women, relegated to only a reproductive function, were denied an education.
   b. all male citizens were professional soldiers.
   c. Helots vastly outnumbered Spartans.
   d. the Spartan system maintained a dual monarchy.

10. At the Battle of Marathon
    a. the Persians defeated the Eretrians and enslaved the survivors.
    b. a small Spartan force repeatedly repelled the Persians before finally losing.
    c. the Ionian revolt collapsed from the combined efforts of the Persian infantry and navy.
    d. the outnumbered Athenian hoplites won a dramatic victory over the Persians.

11. The Athenian repeatedly elected general during the fifth century B.C.E. was _____.
    a. Themistocles
    b. Solon
    c. Cleisthenes
    d. Pericles

12. Greek drama is most associated with festivals that honor the god _____.
    a. Dionysus
    b. Zeus
    c. Apollo
    d. Athena

13. Athenian women
    a. were the most liberated in all of Greece.
    b. were generally restricted to the home.
    c. frequently participated in athletic events.
    d. played an active role in the political affairs of the polis.

14. The Peloponnesian War
    a. saw the rise to power of Athens' greatest leaders.
    b. led Pericles to order an invasion of Syracuse in Sicily.
    c. featured Greece's best naval power versus its best infantry.
    d. allowed the Persians to successfully invade mainland Greece.

15. The phrase "the unexamined life is not worth living" is most associated with _____.
    a. Pericles
    b. Pythagoras
    c. Socrates
    d. Lysander

MATCHING

1. Miletus
2. Aeschylus
3. Parthenon
4. Socrates
5. Sappho
6. Peisistratos
7. Helot
8. Xerxes
9. Homer
10. Delphi

a. tyrant who strengthened the demos in Athens
b. condemned to death for corrupting the youth of Athens
c. author of the *Iliad* and the *Odyssey*
d. site where Apollo's priestess offers advice
e. added characters to present human conflict on stage
f. Ionian land of the Pre-Socratics
g. a Spartan slave
h. temple honoring Athena
i. Persian emperor who invaded Greece
j. a lyric poet

TRUE/FALSE

1. The Greeks modified the Phoenician alphabet by converting some consonants to vowels.
2. The Sophist Protagoras rigorously questioned myths to discover eternal truths.
3. A Greek colony was politically dependent on its mother city.
4. Greek tyrants were usually farmers who had been dispossessed of their land and political power.
5. The lyric poet Archilochus embodied the ideal qualities of a Spartan soldier.
6. The *gerousia* served as Sparta's main court of law.
7. Pre-Socratic philosophers developed rational theories to explain the physical world.
8. The Persians first invaded Greece as revenge for mainland Greek support for the Ionian Revolt.
9. Pericles extended Athenian democracy by allowing citizens to propose and amend legislation.
10. The comedies of Aristophanes often ridiculed important Athenian officials.

PUT THE FOLLOWING ITEMS IN CHRONOLOGICAL ORDER

1. Battle of Salamis   _____
2. Battle of Thermopylae   _____
3. Ionian Revolt   _____
4. Spartan conquest of Messenia _____
5. Battle of Marathon   _____
6. Solon elected archon   _____
7. Death of Socrates   _____
8. Pericles first elected general _____

SHORT ANSWER AND ESSAY QUESTIONS

A. Emergence of Greece

1. Begin by listing the assumptions and values that distinguished the Greeks from their Near Eastern neighbors who were examined in the first two chapters.

2. What marked the end of the Dark Age in Greece?

3. What were the conditions that produced the polis? How do you describe a polis?

4. What were the various reasons behind the foundation of colonies and what were the results of colonization?

5. What kinds of government were found in the poleis? How did these change over time?

6. What were the unique characteristics of Lyric poets? What do lyric poets reveal about the place of an individual in this culture?

B. Compare the major poleis: Athens, Sparta and Miletus

1. Describe the political system as it developed in Athens.

2. Describe the economic base for Athens and the changes that occurred from the early period through the political changes in the state. How were these connected?

3. Use a chart to lay out the development of the political system and then make a parallel chart of the economic basis.

4. What were the basic characteristics of Sparta?

5. Describe Sparta's political system. How did it come about?

7. How was Sparta's society regulated?

8. What was Sparta's "fatal flaw"?

9. What characteristics are valued in the selection *Greek Guest Friendship and Heroic Ideals*?

10. What is the point Herodotus makes in *Yhrasyboulos on How to be a Tyrant* to illustrate how to be a tyrant?

11. Locate Miletus on a map. How did this location differ from Athens and Sparta? How did this affect its development and role in the Hellenic culture?

12. The first philosophical examinations came in Miletus. What made the views of these thinkers unique?

13. Compare and contrast the cities of Athens, Sparta, and Miletus in terms of their economies and development.

C. The Persian wars

1. What were the factors that contributed to the Persian Wars in the following areas: Milites, Persia's ruler (Darius) and Athens?

2. What were the stages of the Persian War?

D. The development of the Golden Age of classical Greece

1. Athens, as the leader of the Delian League, developed in a different way from other states in the league. What were the characteristics of Athens and its relationship to the league's other members?

2. Pericles' power brought what changes to Athens and its democracy?

3. Since drama was an innovation that developed in Athens, examine its stages of development and the characteristics and themes of the plays. How were these a means of political commentary?

4. How did sculpture reveal Greek ideals of human dignity and freedom?

5. Describe sophism using *Two Views of Sophism* as examples to illustrate the various characteristics.

6. What were the various levels of society? What were the duties of each of these groups?

7. The development of Greek philosophy was one of the major contributions of the Classical Age of Greece. Explain the basic ideas of each of the following philosophers: Pythagoras, Protagoras and Socrates.

8. Who were the major Greek playwrights? What themes were presented in their works?

MULTIPLE CHOICE KEY

1. c
2. d
3. b
4. b
5. b
6. c
7. a
8. c
9. a
10. d
11. d
12. a
13. b
14. c
15. c

MATCHING KEY

1. f
2. e
3. h
4. b
5. j
6. a
7. g
8. i
9. c
10. d

TRUE/FALSE KEY

1. T
2. F
3. F
4. F
5. F
6. T
7. T
8. T
9. T
10. T

CHRONOLOGICAL ORDER KEY

4, 6, 3, 5, 2, 1, 8, 7

CHAPTER 4 | The Expansion of Greece

This chapter focuses on the period of the Greeks known as the Hellenistic Age, an era defined by the appearance of Greek-like culture. You will need to know how this period was similar to and different from the earlier Greek (Hellenic) period. As you work through the exercises and the questions, think about how the changes in philosophy, sculpture, and society are responses to changes in politics. While you are working through the study questions, keep in mind the broader question: "What are the changes from the earlier period?"

CHAPTER OUTLINE

1. Introduction

2. Failures of the fourth-century polis
   a. The struggle for hegemony
   b. Social and economic crises

3. The cultural and intellectual response
   a. Art and literature
   b. Philosophy and political thought in the age of Plato and Aristotle
      i. Plato's philosophical system
      ii. Aristotelian thought
      iii. Xenophon and Isocrates
   c. The rise of Macedon and the conquests of Alexander
      i. The reign of Philip II (359–336 B.C.E.)
      ii. The conquests and reign of Alexander (336–323 B.C.E.)
   d. The Hellenistic kingdoms
      i. Ptolemaic Egypt
      ii. Seleucid Asia
      iii. Antigonid Macedon and Greece
   e. The growth of trade and urbanization
   f. Hellenistic culture: philosophy and religion
      i. Epicureanism and Stoicism
      ii. Skepticism
      iii. Religion
   g. Hellenistic culture: literature and art
      i. Pastoral literature
      ii. Prose
      iii. Architecture
      iv. Sculpture
   h. Science and Medicine
      i. Astronomy, mathematics, and geography
      ii. Medicine
   i. The transformation of the polis

4. Conclusion

IDENTIFY

1. Epaminondas
2. Greek mercenaries
3. Hellenistic
4. Menander
5. Plato
6. Aristotle
7. Xenophon
8. Philip II
9. Demosthenes
10. Alexander
11. Ptolemies
12. Seleucids
13. Antigonids
14. Epicureanism
15. Stoicism
16. Skepticism
17. Mystery Cults
18. Polybius
19. Mithraism
20. Euclid

MULTIPLE CHOICE

1. At the Battle of Leuctra
   a. Argos, Athens, and Corinth united to defeat Sparta.
   b. Athens and the reestablished Delian League united Greece.
   c. Thebes defeated Sparta.
   d. the Messenians overwhelmed the Spartans to end centuries of enslavement.

2. Menander's writings
   a. increasingly focused on political and social themes.
   b. reflected the growing pessimism associated with the decline of the polis.
   c. tended to be escapist with stories of mistaken identities and comedic misunderstandings.
   d. praised Philip II as the savior of Greece.

3. In *The Republic*, Plato stated that
   a. one must use his senses to understand true virtue.
   b. order and social harmony would be best achieved by a government controlled by philospher-kings.
   c. democracy was the highest form of political development.
   d. a system of checks and balances would prevent the spread of tyranny.

4. Demosthenes
   a. viewed Philip II as a threat to Greek independence.
   b. welcomed Philip II as a savior who ended an age of inter-Greek warfare.
   c. unsuccessfully led the Greek army at the Battle of Chaeronea.
   d. challenged Plato's world of Ideas and Forms.

5. Philip II's Companions
   a. was his cohort of military advisers who planned the invasion of Persia.
   b. were the philosophers/tutors who educated the young Alexander.
   c. was his best armed and best disciplined phalanx.
   d. was his elite cavalry squad.

6. During the Hellenistic Age, Alexandria was
   a. the capital of the Ptolemaic kingdom.
   b. the largest Hellenistic city.
   c. the most important city of learning and scholarship.
   d. all of the above.

7. Epicureans
   a. promoted pleasure as the highest good.
   b. regarded virtue as an end in itself.
   c. denied the doctrine of free will.
   d. promoted the contemplative life to discover absolute justice.

8. All of the following are true concerning Mithraism except
   a. December twenty-fifth was the holiest day honoring the god.
   b. the religion grew out of Zoroastrianism.
   c. like Dionysus, Mithras was never thought to have lived a human life.
   d. it became one of the important religions in the Roman world.

9. The historian who developed a cyclical view of history in which nations passed through stages of growth and decline was _____.
   a. Theocritus
   b. Zeno of Athens
   c. Polybius
   d. Xenophon

10. Hellenistic sculpture emphasized
    a. traditional Greek ideals of modesty and simplicity.
    b. extreme naturalism and extravagance.
    c. a return to poses and postures that were Egyptian in origin.
    d. none of the above.

MATCHING

1. Epominandas
2. Philip II
3. Alexander
4. Aristotle
5. Zeno
6. Euclid
7. Erastosthenes
8. Aristarchus
9. Archimedes
10. Herophilus

a. believed the earth revolved around the sun
b. considered the brain to be the center of intelligence
c. wrote *Elements of Geometry*
d. victorious at Gaugamela
e. calculated the circumference of the earth to within 200 miles
f. believed in the objective reality of material things
g. greatest technical genius of the ancient world
h. Theban military genius
i. victorious at Chaeronea
j. founder of Stoicism

TRUE/FALSE

1. During the Hellenistic Age, economic problems prompted many Greeks to become mercenaries.

2. Plato believed that what our senses perceived was true reality.

3. Alexander's conquests extended from Egypt into India.

4. Rulers who patronized the sciences were unconcerned with the prestige that might accompany new advances.

5. Prosperity in the Hellenistic world was, in large part, based on the growth of long-distance trade.

6. Industrial production was the primary source of wealth in the Hellenistic world.

7. Hellenistic monarchs generally respected the political and cultural independence of poleis within their borders.

8. Mystery cults offered the possibility of salvation through a personal savior.

9. True skeptics denied that all knowledge was relative and instead insisted that sense perception, if properly channeled, could discern absolute truth.

10. The Ptolemies learned to speak Egyptian to gain the support of the lower classes.

PUT THE FOLLOWING ITEMS IN CHRONOLOGICAL ORDER

1. Battle of Gaugamela   _____

2. Death of Alexander   _____

3. Battle of Chaeronea   _____

4. Battle of Leuctra   _____

5. Death of Philip II   _____

SHORT ANSWER AND ESSAY QUESTIONS

A. Political changes in the Greek city-states, i.e. the poleis.

1. Show how alliances between and among the poleis kept shifting so that total unity or hegemony was impossible.

2. What were the reasons behind the breakdown of the poleis?

3. What were the reasons behind the decline in the standard of living?

B. Drama and philosophy

1. What were the reasons for the audiences' attendance at plays? How did the arts (drama and sculpture) reflect a new approach?

2. What was the goal of the philosophers? What were they trying to obtain and what were they trying to provide?

3. Aristotle believed in a balance in philosophical ideas. Give examples of this concept of balance in his philosophy.

4. How did Plato approach political ideas? What was his interpretation?

5. Both Plato and Aristotle recognized there were problems in the polis. What was new or different in the ways other philophers looked at these problems?

C. The rise of Macedonian power

1. Trace Philip II's rise to power. What were the steps he took and how did this secure the position of Macedon?

2. Read the two views of Philip II in the textbook. Which writer is favorable? Which writer is unfavorable? Why did you reach that conclusion?

3. Philip II's son Alexander succeeded his father. How did he increase the power of Macedon?

4. After Alexander's death, the territory he had conquered was divided into three parts. Where were these three parts? How were they similar and how did they differ? A good way to approach this is to make a chart of each area.

D. The economic, philosophical, social, and religious changes of the Hellenistic period

1. Describe the economic and social effects of the larger political states of the Hellenistic world. How were these different from the earlier Hellenic period?

2. What were the objectives of the Hellenistic philosophers? How were Epicurean and Stoic philosophies similar in these goals?

3. How were the Epicureans and the Stoics different? To approach these questions list the characteristics of the Stoics and then the characteristics of the Epicureans.

4. The Skeptics offered another view of philosophy. How would you describe their view of knowledge? How could this be defined as extreme?

5. How were philosophy and religion reactions against the extremes in Hellenistic society?

6. As discussed in *The Greek Influence of Israel,* what were some of the things done in Jerusalem that illustrate this influence?

E. Hellenistic culture

1. What was pastoral literature? What was the reason behind it? Find an example to illustrate this in *Escape to the Countryside* by Theocritus.

2. How were art and literature reactions against the economic and political extremes in Hellenistic society?

3. How are the aspects of culture a reaction to the new political world?

4. What are the main characteristics of the architectural style?

5. What are the characteristics of Hellenistic sculpture?

F. Hellenistic science and medicine

1. What were the new scientific advances?

2. What were the medical achievements of Herophilus? Erasistratus?

3. What were the reasons behind these advances?

G. What were the contributions of Hellenistic culture to Western civilization?

MATCHING KEY

1. h
2. i
3. d
4. f
5. j
6. c
7. e
8. a
9. g
10. b

TRUE/FALSE KEY

1. T
2. F
3. T
4. F
5. T
6. F
7. F
8. T
9. F
10. F

CHRONOLOGICAL ORDER KEY

4, 3, 5, 1, 2

MULTIPLE CHOICE KEY

1. c
2. c
3. b
4. a
5. d
6. d
7. a
8. c
9. c
10. b

CHAPTER 5 | Roman Civilization

As you study this chapter you will need to explore Roman ideals as they reflect their traditional view of society. Roman civilization existed for a long time and part of your exercises will involve dividing the development into its various stages, beginning with early Rome, the Roman Republic, and the Roman Empire. Throughout this period, the characteristics of Roman civilization and its society remained traditional. As you read through this chapter, keep in mind the question, "What were the traditional values of the Romans?"

CHAPTER OUTLINE

1. Introduction

2. Early Italy and the Roman monarchy
   a. The Etruscans
   b. The rise of Rome

3. The early republic
   a. The government of the early republic
   b. Culture, religion, and morality

4. The fateful wars with Carthage
   a. Territorial expansion

5. Society and culture in the late republic
   a. Economic and social change
   b. Family life and the status of women
   c. Epicureanism and Stoicism
   d. Religion

6. The social struggles of the late republic
   a. The Gracchi
   b. Aristocratic reaction
   c. Pompey and Julius Caesar

7. The Principate or early empire (27 B.C.E.–180 C.E.)
   a. The Augustan settlement of government
   b. Romanization and assimilation

8. Culture and life in the period of the Principate
   a. Literature of the Golden and Silver Ages
   b. Art and architecture
   c. Aristocratic women under the Principate
   d. Gladiatorial combats
   e. New religions
   f. Roman law
   g. The economy of Italy during the Principate

9. The Crisis of the third century (180–284 C.E.)
   a. The Severan Dynasty
   b. The height of the Third-Century Crisis
   c. Neoplatonism

10. Roman rule in the west: the balance sheet
    a. Explaining the decline and fall of Rome
    b. Political failures
    c. Economic crises
    d. Roman achievements

11. Conclusion

IDENTIFY

1. Latin Right
2. Senate
3. consuls
4. patricians
5. plebeians
6. Equestrian Order
7. Roman religion
8. Punic wars
9. Roman slavery
10. Lucretius
11. Cicero
12. the Gracchi
13. Marius
14. Caesar
15. Principate

16. "Five Good Emperors"
17. Virgil
18. Roman Law
19. Neoplatonism
20. fall of Rome

MULTIPLE CHOICE

1. Which of the following is not true regarding the Etruscans?
   a. They were Indo-Europeans whose language resembled Greek.
   b. Etruscan women held a surprisingly elevated status for their time.
   c. Their gods appeared in human form.
   d. Gladiatorial contests originated in Etruscan society.

2. Roman consuls
   a. were elected military leaders who served for life and often transferred their power to their sons.
   b. represented the conservative, royal element in the government of the early republic.
   c. generally came from all groups in Roman society to strengthen loyalty to Rome.
   d. represented the most democratic element of the Roman government.

3. The Struggle of the Orders refers to the
   a. series of battles that led to the eventual collapse of Etruscan civilization.
   b. conflicts that emerged between the Romans and Greeks when the Romans attempted to become a commercial and naval power.
   c. two-centuries-long clash between patricians and plebeians over political rights.
   d. political clash between the consuls and Senate over control of the military.

4. Publius Cornelius Scipio earned the title "Africanus"
   a. after marrying Cleopatra and incorporating Egypt into the Roman empire.
   b. through his appointment as consul for North Africa following the Third Punic War.
   c. for defeating Hannibal at Zama and ending the Second Punic War.
   d. for his use of a mercenary army of Egyptians to conquer Greece and Macedonia.

5. A major economic consequence of the Roman Republic's wars of conquest was
   a. the strengthening of the financial position of small farmers who now gained additional land and wealth.
   b. the impoverishment of many small farmers who could no longer compete with slave labor on large agricultural estates.
   c. a reduction in the number of slaves in Italy as the Latin Right was extended to Greeks and Macedonians.
   d. a reduction in the economic standing of the Equestrians because the Romans relied less and less on cavalry forces.

6. Lucretius' *On the Nature of Things*
   a. admonished young Romans to remain faithful to household deities.
   b. stressed the cruel and impulsive nature of the Roman gods.
   c. denied the existence of the gods and the afterlife.
   d. sought to reduce the average Roman's fear of the supernatural world.

7. Stoicism
   a. influenced Romans such as Cicero to conclude that mental tranquility was the highest good.
   b. influenced not only the writings of Plautus, but the poems of Catullus as well.
   c. had a negligible effect on Rome until it was embraced by many third-century emperors.
   d. blended with Epicureanism to form a new philosophical outlook called Neoplatonism.

8. The reforms of the Gracchi sought to
   a. reduce social and economic problems through land reform.
   b. address potential manpower shortages in the Roman military.
   c. extend Roman citizenship to all Italians.
   d. all of the above.

9. All of the following are true of Caesar except
   a. he initially allied with Pompey to control Rome.
   b. he generally respected the independence of the Senate while serving as dictator.
   c. he extended citizenship to many non-Italians.
   d. his "Julian" calendar served western Europe for centuries.

10. Historians generally regard the Roman empire as beginning with the reign of _____.
    a. Caesar
    b. Claudius
    c. Tiberius
    d. Augustus

11. All of the following ruled during the era of the "Five Good Emperors except _____.
    a. Marius
    b. Trajan
    c. Nerva
    d. Hadrian

12. Virgil's *Aeneid*
    a. offers the first glimpses of the uncivilized world of the German barbarians.
    b. is a patriotic epic recounting the founding of Rome by a Trojan warrior.
    c. is the source for stories of Cincinnatus and Horatius.
    d. none of the above.

13. Roman advances in engineering include _____.
    a. roads
    b. bridges
    c. aqueducts
    d. all of the above

14. Roman aristocratic women
    a. were excluded from owning property and participating in business activities.
    b. were under constant male supervision when outside of the home.
    c. sometimes engaged in literary and intellectual pursuits.
    d. had less sexual freedom than their counterparts in Greece.

15. According to the text, the most legitimate explanations for the "fall" of Rome include
    a. economic consequences associated with a reliance on slavery and persistent problems over imperial succession.
    b. conquest by German "barbarians" intent on destroying the achievements of Roman civilization.
    c. lead poisoning and corruption of traditional morals.
    d. both a and b.

MATCHING

1. Hannibal
2. Plotinus
3. Marius
4. Pompey
5. Tacitus
6. *colonni*
7. *latifundia*
8. *princeps*
9. Actium
10. Spartacus

a. semi-servile farm workers
b. gladiator and slave revolt leader
c. Caesar's rival for control of Rome
d. allowed the poor and property-less to serve in the Roman military
e. Augustus' preferred title
f. Carthaginian military genius
g. respected the masculine virtues of the Germans
h. Octavian's victory over Antony and Cleopatra
i. large agricultural estates
j. promoted asceticism to achieve mystic reunion with the divine

TRUE/FALSE

1. Sulla's dictatorship eliminated any possibility of strengthening senatorial powers.
2. During the Principate, the Senate remained the leading authority in Rome.
3. Livy and Ovid were two of Rome's greatest historians.
4. Wall paintings and mosaics were the Romans' most original art forms.
5. Roman law contained elements of natural law including concepts affirming the equality of all men.
6. The Severan ruler Caracalla's acceptance of Stoic philosophy prompted his actions extending Roman citizenship.
7. The *concilium plebis* eventually emerged as an important legislative body in the Roman Republic.
8. Traditional Roman religion included ancestor worship.
9. The growth of slavery benefited wealthy women by freeing them from some traditional roles.
10. Augustus promoted traditional morality by limiting divorce and punishing adultery.

PUT THE FOLLOWING ITEMS IN CHRONOLOGICAL ORDER

1. Second Punic War _____
2. Death of Caesar _____
3. Period of the Gracchi _____
4. Marius becomes consul _____
5. Battle of Actium _____

SHORT ANSWER AND ESSAY QUESTIONS

A. The early years of Roman society

1. What were the contributions of the Etruscans to Roman civilization?
2. How did geography influence Rome? First examine the geography of the area and then assess its influence on the societies on the Italian peninsula.

3. What was the Latin Right and why was it important in the expansion of Rome?

4. As the Roman state grew in size, what were its characteristics? How did these characteristics—virtues—contribute to the expansion?

5. How does the reading in the textbook on "The Rape of Lucretia" illustrate Roman values? What were these values?

B. The growth of the Roman state and government

1. The government of Rome developed into a republic. What was the structure of this government?

2. Initially the plebeians were not part of the government structure.
   a. What were the grievances of the plebeians?
   b. How did the Law of the Twelve Tables help the plebeians?

3. How do a monarchy and a republic differ?

4. Explain how religion was part of the government. What was the Roman interpretation of religion?

C. The Punic Wars

1. Looking at the maps of the Greek colonial world and the Phoenicians' colonial territory, what do you notice about their correlation to each other?

2. With the Punic Wars, Rome established a new policy toward conquered peoples. This was first apparent within Sicily. What was this new policy?

3. How did the economic base change with the expansion of territory under the Romans?

4. How was society changed with the establishment of control over such a large territory? What were the new groups of people in the structure of the state? What did the people in these new groups do?

5. Why did Rome not progress with new mechanical inventions or innovations?

D. Religion, women, and philosophy

1. How was the late republic affected by Greek philosophical ideals of Stoicism and Epicureanism? What did the Romans contribute to these philosophies?

2. How did the Romans add new religious views with the spread of mystery cults yet still maintain the traditional practice of Roman religion?

E. Responses of the Romans

1. How did the Gracchi brothers try to deal with the social and economic changes?

2. How did Marius' changes in military qualifications change the traditional soldiers' view of loyalty?

3. How did these military changes affect the traditional social views?

4. One source of change was the luxuries from the Greeks. Using the reading in the textbook on *Greek Luxury,* list some of these luxuries.

5. Julius Caesar, at the end of the period of the Roman Republic, made several changes in various areas of Roman life. What were some of these changes?

F. The Principate

1. What is the beginning of the Roman empire?

2. What are the various stages of Roman government under the empire?

3. To assess Augustus, consider his contributions to government by listing the various ways he presented himself in order to appear "traditional" to the Roman value system.

4. In order to compare views of Augustus, read the "Two View of Augustus' Rule" in the textbook before considering the following questions.
   a. How does Augustus explain what he has done in government?
   b. How does Tacitus, writing later, view Augustus?

5. How were the peoples in the provinces of the Empire treated by the center of power in Rome?

6. How was Stoic philosophy viewed during the Principate?

7. What were the two divisions of Principate literature? What are the characteristics of each?

8. What were the various variations of Roman art? What were the different ways it was used?

9. How did the role of women in the upper class of society change during the early stages of the empire?

10. How do you think the deification of emperors was connected to traditional Roman values?

G. Roman law

1. Examine the development of Roman law by tracing the various kinds of law, beginning with the Latin Right and continuing through the republic and the empire.

2. What was the major contribution of the Principate to Roman law?

3. What changes to the law came with the Roman empire? Why did these come about?

4. What were the divisions of law in its three branches?

5. What made "Natural Law" unique?

H. The Third-Century Crisis

1. What problems developed during the Third-Century Crisis?

2. What was the response to this crisis? Did this help?

3. Why is neo-Platonism at odds with the traditional values of the Roman state?

4. What were the crucial problems to the continuation of the Roman empire?

I. At the end of this chapter, consider the contributions of the Roman state to Western civilization.

MATCHING KEY

1. f
2. j
3. d
4. c
5. g
6. a
7. i
8. e
9. h
10. b

TRUE/FALSE KEY

1. F
2. F
3. F
4. T
5. T
6. F
7. T
8. T
9. T
10. T

CHRONOLOGICAL ORDER KEY

1, 3, 4, 2, 5

MULTIPLE CHOICE KEY

1. a
2. b
3. c
4. c
5. b
6. d
7. a
8. d
9. b
10. d
11. a
12. b
13. d
14. c
15. a

CHAPTER 6

Christianity and the Transformation of the Roman World

The focus of this chapter is the division of the Roman empire between its eastern and western halves and the development of new cultures that redefined what it meant to be Roman. This division ended the Classical Period and provided a link to the medieval world. The chapter also examines the growth of Christianity and how it transformed the empire, and forces outside of the Roman empire that contributed to this transformation.

CHAPTER OUTLINE

1. Introduction

2. The reorganized empire
   a. The reign of Diocletian
   b. The reign of Constantine

3. The emergence and triumph of Christianity
   a. The career of Jesus
   b. Jesus and Second Temple Judaism
   c. The growth of Christianity in the Hellenistic world
   d. Christianity and the Roman empire

4. The new contours of fourth-century Christianity
   a. Doctrinal quarrels
   b. The spread of monasticism
   c. Changing attitudes toward women, marriage, and the body

5. The Germanic invasions and the fall of the western Roman empire
   a. German-Roman relations
   b. The success and impact of Germanic invasions

6. The shaping of Western Christian thought
   a. Saint Jerome and Saint Ambrose

   b. The life and thought of Saint Augustine
   c. Boethius links classical and medieval thought

7. The Christianization of classical culture in the West
   a. Cassiodorus and the Benedictine tradition of learning

8. Eastern Rome and the western empire
   a. Justinian's revival of the Roman empire
   b. The codification of Roman law
   c. Justinian's military conquests
   d. The impact of Justinian's reconquest on the western Roman empire

9. Conclusion

IDENTIFY

1. Diocletian
2. Constantine
3. Theodosius I
4. Jesus
5. Pharisees
6. Essenes
7. Zealots
8. Saul of Tarsus
9. Arius
10. Bishop of Rome
11. Saint Benedict
12. Visigoths
13. Ostrogoths
14. Saint Jerome
15. Saint Ambrose
16. Saint Augustine
17. Saint Gregory the Great

18. Boethius
19. Theodoric
20. Justinian

MULTIPLE CHOICE

1. Diocletian's tetrarchy
   a. was designed to stem the tide of barbarian invasions.
   b. provided a rational system for imperial succession.
   c. ended imperial succession disputes once and for all.
   d. was an effort to stabilize Rome's currency.

2. Constantinople
   a. was founded in 324 as Rome's new capital.
   b. was home to Diocletian's retirement palace.
   c. was poorly situated for trade and communications but was well situated for defensive purposes.
   d. both a and b

3. Milan, Ravenna, and Trier
   a. were major manufacturing centers in the western Roman world.
   b. were centers of secessionist tendencies within the Roman empire.
   c. increasingly served as imperial residences in the West.
   d. fell to the Visigoths shortly after the reign of Theodosius.

4. According to the text, Jesus' contemporaries probably regarded him as a Pharisee because of
   a. his belief in life after death.
   b. his admonitions to follow the spirit of the law.
   c. his emphasis on the ethical requirements of the law.
   d. all of the above.

5. At the Battle of Milvian Bridge
   a. Theodosius I slaughtered thousands of pagans.
   b. Julian the Apostate died at the hands of the Persians.
   c. Constantine's forces fought with a Christian symbol painted on their shields.
   d. none of the above.

6. Emperor Theodosius the Great
   a. divided the Roman empire between his sons.
   b. banned pagan worship throughout the Roman empire.
   c. was the last pagan emperor of Rome.
   d. both a and b

7. Arius was declared a heretic because he
   a. denied that Christ was co-eternal with the father and of the same substance.
   b. denied that Christ was the son of God.
   c. declared that Christ was both God the Father and the Holy Ghost.
   d. questioned the salvation of the soul.

8. The key figure in the development of monasticism in western Europe was _____.
   a. Saint Basil
   b. Saint Augustine
   c. Saint Benedict
   d. Saint Ambrose

9. Saint Jerome's greatest legacy was his
   a. insistence that the pope ruled the entire Christian world.
   b. translation of the Bible into Latin.
   c. denial of the spiritual importance of monasticism.
   d. complete rejection of the classics of Roman literature.

10. In *On the City of God*, Saint Augustine
    a. stressed a doctrine of predestination.
    b. suggested Christians should live according to the standards of the "City of Man".
    c. reminded Christians that their thoughts and actions should reflect a desire to reach the "City of God".
    d. both a and c

11. All of the following are true regarding Boethius except
    a. he has been called the "last of the Romans".
    b. his *Consolation of Philosophy* taught that human happiness could only be achieved through God.
    c. his *Confessions* recounted his journey from his sinful nature to his acceptance of Christianity.
    d. his handbooks on arithmetic and music summarized what Christians should know about those subjects.

12. _____ was author of the *Institutes* and the *History of the Goths* and stressed classical learning to ensure proper Biblical understanding.
    a. Benedict
    b. Saint Jerome
    c. Cassiodorus
    d. Saint Augustine

13. All of the following are true of Theodoric except
    a. he was essentially a Romanized ruler.
    b. he persecuted Arian Christians.
    c. he provided Italy with an enlightened government not seen for several centuries.
    d. both Cassiodorus and Boethius worked at his court.

14. Justinian's most lasting achievement was his
    a. codification of Roman law.
    b. conquest of the western Roman empire.
    c. insistence on classical learning for all Christians.
    d. none of the above.

15. Justinian's conquests included all of the following parts of the western Roman empire except_____.
    a. Gaul
    b. Spain
    c. northwest Africa
    d. Italy

MATCHING

1. Dominus
2. Byzantium
3. Aelia Capitolina
4. Torah
5. Paul
6. Galerius
7. Visigoths
8. Ostrogoths
9. Ambrose
10. Belarius

a. established a kingdom in Italy
b. conquered the kingdom of the Vandals in Africa
c. prompted Theodosius to perform penance
d. issued an edict of toleration for Christians in 311
e. site used to establish Constantinople
f. first five books of the Hebrew Bible
g. founded on the ruins of Jerusalem
h. Diocletian's title
i. defeated the Romans at the Battle of Adrianople
j. the apostle to the Gentiles

TRUE/FALSE

1. Diocletian's reforms included the creation of two augusti and two caesars.
2. Crucifixion was the typical verdict for those found guilty of sedition against Rome.
3. According to the text, historians are certain about the reasons people converted to Christianity.
4. During the second and third centuries, Jewish legal scholars relied heavily on Christian interpretations in their writings.
5. During the first two centuries, Roman authorities largely tolerated Christians.
6. With the growth of asceticism, Christian thinkers increasingly associated women with sins of the flesh.
7. The church regarded virginity as the highest ideal for women but not for men.
8. The Germanic invasions brought an immediate end to Roman culture in the West.
9. For Augustine, humans appeared to be naturally inclined to commit wicked acts.
10. Christian intellectuals were unconcerned with being considered philosophers because their sole purpose was spiritual perfection.

PUT THE FOLLOWING ITEMS IN CHRONOLOGICAL ORDER

1. Battle of Milvian Bridge _____
2. Justinian becomes emperor _____
3. Battle of Adrianople _____
4. Conversion of Saul of Tarsus _____
5. Discovery of the Dead Sea Scrolls _____

SHORT ANSWER AND ESSAY QUESTIONS

A. Political

1. What were the three major cultural trends that characterized the world of late antiquity?
2. What did Diocletian do to change the image of the emperor? Why did he make these changes?
3. Explain how and why power shifted to the eastern half of the empire.
4. What were the political and economic changes made by Diocletian?

B. Early Christianity

1. What were the stages in the growth of Christianity?
2. Trace the career of Jesus and explain his ideals.
3. How do various writings provide an understanding of the career and ideals of Jesus?
4. What were the various Jewish groups at the time of Jesus? What were the goals of these groups?
5. How was this new religion spread to non-Jews? What was the appeal of the religion?
6. Explain what caused the split between Jews and Christians during the second and third centuries.
7. What do you learn from *Emperor Trajan's letter to Pliny the Elder* about persecution of Christians in the Roman era? What was the government's usual approach to the Christians in this period?

C. Christianity accepted

1. What were the major changes to Christianity during the fourth century? Why do you think these occurred?

2. Explain how the roots of the pope's claim to primacy over the Christian church in the West were rooted in the fifth century. How was this related to the political situation at the time?

3. What was monasticism? Explain the reasons for its appeal as a response to the anxieties of the age.

4. What were the different kinds of monasticism? How did these develop?

5. Compare the Christian view of women in the early centuries and the view of women beginning in the fourth century.

6. Compare and contrast the two selections in *Changing Attitudes toward the Celibacy of Bishops*. What is this fourth-century change in attitude? How does this relate to the preceding question?

D. Germanic invasions

1. How did Romans view Germans? Why was this the case?

2. What were the reasons for the success of Germanic forces in the West?

3. Using the selections in *Romanized Barbarians and Barbarianized Romans,* explain how the Romans and the Barbarians influenced each other.

E. Theological and intellectual thought

1. Examine the contributions of the four great Fathers of the Western church. What did they contribute that was new to Christianity?

2. Examine the views of St. Augustine and explain what they were and his basis for them.

3. How does Boethius provide a link between classical and medieval intellectuals?

4. How were classical traditions in learning adapted by the Christians? What were the two forms that were used?

5. What was the Arian view of Christianity in both 325 and 523 C.E.? Why are those two dates significant?

6. Explain why Boethius' execution was such an important historical turning point.

F. Late political development

1. What was the emperor Justinian's goal? How did he try to achieve this?

2. What was Justinian's major contribution? Explain what it was and why it was important.

3. What were the divisions of the Italian areas?

4. Explain how these changes affected the eastern and western halves of the empire in their sense of being Roman.

MULTIPLE CHOICE KEY

1. b
2. a
3. c
4. d
5. c
6. d
7. a
8. c
9. b
10. d
11. c
12. c
13. b
14. a
15. a

MATCHING KEY

1. h
2. e
3. g
4. f
5. j
6. d
7. i
8. a
9. c
10. b

TRUE/FALSE KEY

1. T
2. T
3. F
4. F
5. T
6. T
7. F
8. F
9. T
10. F

CHRONOLOGICAL ORDER KEY

4, 1, 3, 2, 5

CHAPTER 7 | Rome's Three Heirs: The Byzantine, Islamic, and Early Medieval Worlds

The focus of this chapter is the development of three different cultures from the earlier Roman empire. As you study, think about things that change and those that remain the same in terms of religion, literature, and economics.

CHAPTER OUTLINE

1. Introduction

2. The Byzantine empire and its culture
   a. Sources of stability
   b. Byzantine religion
   c. Byzantine culture
   d. Byzantium and the western Christian world

3. The growth of Islam
   a. The rise of Islam
   b. The religious teachings of Islam
   c. The Islamic conquests
   d. The Shiite-Sunni schism
   e. Umayyad and Abbasids

4. The changing Islamic world
   a. Muslim society and culture
      i. Muslim philosophy, science, and medicine
      ii. Literature and art
      iii. Trade and industry
   b. The impact of early Islamic civilization on Europe

5. Western Christian civilization in the early Middle Ages
   a. Economic disintegration and political instability
   b. Merovingian Gaul
      i. Monasticism and conversion
      ii. The reign of Pope Gregory I

6. The rise of the Carolingians
   a. The reign of Charlemagne
   b. Christianity and kingship
   c. The Carolingian renaissance
   d. Charlemagne and the revival of the western Roman empire
   e. The collapse of the Carolingians
   f. The legacy of the Carolingians

7. Conclusion

IDENTIFY

1. Byzantine
2. Leo the Isaurian
3. Seljuk Turks
4. Iconoclastic Controversy
5. Muhammad
6. Mecca
7. Hijrah
8. Qur'an
9. Shiites
10. Sunnis
11. Averroes
12. Umar Khayyam
13. Maimonides
14. Gregory of Tours
15. Clovis
16. Charles Martel
17. Saint Boniface
18. Charlemagne
19. Alfred the Great
20. Otto I

MULTIPLE CHOICE

1. According to the text, Byzantine history begins with the reign of _____.
   a. Justinian
   b. Constantine
   c. Heraclius
   d. Diocletian

2. Among the reasons for the success of the Byzantine state were
   a. its efficient bureaucracy.
   b. its comparatively sound economic base.
   c. its impressive army, navy, and diplomatic corps.
   d. all of the above.

3. Iconoclasts
   a. wanted to prevent the worship of images of Christ and the saints.
   b. eventually triumphed in the ninth century.
   c. demanded that Christian art respond to the spiritual ideals of Islamic art.
   d. reflected the traditional view of Christian art.

4. One of the striking features of Byzantine intellectual life was
   a. the dominant role that the classics of Roman thought played in educational institutions.
   b. the rejection of most of the literary masterpieces of ancient Greece.
   c. the relatively large number of educated women in comparison to other civilizations of the time.
   d. both a and c

5. All of the following are true of Muhammad except
   a. he was born in Mecca.
   b. he regarded himself as the second coming of Christ.
   c. he considered himself to be the last and greatest prophet of God.
   d. his religious views share similarities with Judaism and Christianity.

6. As a military force, Islam
   a. conquered Constantinople in 717 but could not hold on to it.
   b. conquered much of ancient Persia and the late Roman world less than a century after Muhammad's death.
   c. was defeated by the Visigoths in Spain and North Africa.
   d. forced conquered subjects to convert immediately.

7. The capital of the Umayyads was _____.
   a. Damascus
   b. Baghdad
   c. Istanbul
   d. Mecca

8. A major cause of the decline of the Abbasid caliphate was
   a. repeated military defeats at the hands of the Franks.
   b. inability to establish diplomatic and trade relations with the Franks.
   c. gradual decline of their agricultural wealth in the Tigris-Euphrates basin.
   d. both a and b

9. The two most important influences on medieval Islamic philosophy were
   a. Platonism and Aristotelianism.
   b. Zoroastrianism and Stoicism.
   c. Epicureanism and Stoicism.
   d. Neoplatonism and Aristotelianism.

10. All of the following are accurate regarding Muslim scientists and physicians except
    a. several astronomers believed that the earth moved around the sun.
    b. physicians organized hospitals into separate wards for specific illnesses.
    c. mathematicians combined the geometry of the Greeks with the numbering systems of the Hindus.
    d. all of the above are true

11. The Islamic influence on Western civilization included
    a. new words such as *traffic*, *alcohol*, and *algebra*.
    b. the preservation of Greek thought later translated into Latin.
    c. religious commentaries that inspired Christianity to adopt notions such as purgatory and original sin.
    d. both a and b

12. The founder of the Merovingian Dynasty was _____.
    a. Clovis
    b. Pepin the Short
    c. Charlemagne
    d. Louis the Pious

13. Women frequently joined convents because
    a. it was an honorable position that offered salvation.
    b. of the opportunity to consult with kings and nobles.
    c. of the attraction many had for the guidelines established in the Rule of Saint Benedict.
    d. all of the above.

14. Pope Gregory I is remembered for
    a. writing a new rule book for monks.
    b. promoting the concept of purgatory and stressing the essential role of penance.
    c. crowning Charlemagne emperor of the Franks.
    d. excommunicating the patriarch in Constantinople for refusing to accept papal authority.

15. As king of the Franks, Charlemagne
    a. considered himself leader of a unified Christian realm.

b. traveled widely and appointed *missi* as his personal representatives from his court.

c. changed the liturgy, appointed church officials, enforced Christian practices, and prohibited practices.

d. all of the above.

MATCHING

1. caliph
2. Aachen
3. Leo the Isaurian
4. Homer
5. Santa Sophia
6. Mecca
7. Ali
8. Islam
9. Alfred the Great
10. Leo III

a. best example of Byzantine architecture

b. holiest of Islamic cities

c. deputy of the Prophet

d. a guide for morality and wisdom to the Byzantines

e. borrowed Carolingian political ideas

f. crowned Charlemagne emperor

g. Charlemagne's capital

h. successfully defended Constantinople in 717

i. submission

j. first Shiite caliph

TRUE/FALSE

1. Heraclius' greatest victories came against Islamic forces.

2. Byzantine history is replete with palace revolts involving mutilations, murders, and blindings.

3. One of the striking features of Byzantine Christianity was its ability to avoid conflict over remote religious issues.

4. Muslims regard Jesus as a prophet but not as divine.

5. Today, Shiites make up a majority of Muslims in Iran.

6. Wealthy Muslim men were allowed to have as many as six wives.

7. Al-Ghazzali's commentaries on Aristotle's writings served as the principle influences on Aquinas and Dante.

8. The Battle of Tours halted an Islamic incursion into France.

9. The Carolingian renaissance endorsed classical learning as an essential prerequisite to understanding Christianity.

10. After Charlemagne's death, his empire rapidly collapsed and was divided among his three grandsons.

PUT THE FOLLOWING ITEMS IN CHRONOLOGICAL ORDER

1. Death of Muhammad _____

2. Battle of Tours _____

3. Charlemagne crowned emperor _____

4. Heraclius becomes emperor _____

5. Clovis converts to Christianity _____

SHORT ANSWER AND ESSAY QUESTIONS

A. The Byzantine empire

1. What were the reasons behind the success and longevity of the Byzantine state?

2. What was the Iconoclastic movement? Explain the differing views of why it happened.

3. What was the basic literature of Byzantine education?

4. How does the selection on *Byzantine Classicism* illustrate the sense of continuity the Byzantines felt between their own Christian world and the world of the ancient Greeks?

5. What were the characteristics of the Byzantine educational system?

6. What do the western Europeans owe to the Byzantine empire?

B. The rise of Islam

1. How did Muhammad organize the Islamic religion?

2. What are the basics beliefs of Islam?

3. How is Islam similar to Judaism and Christianity? How is it different?

4. How does the *Pact of Umar* illustrate the relationship between Muslim conquerors and their Christian subjects?

5. Explain the differences between the Shiite and Sunni interpretations of Islam.

6. What was the significance of the Abbasid caliphate to western Europe?

7. What are the various ethnic and political divisions in the Islamic world?

8. What are the reasons behind the original cosmopolitan culture of Islam?

9. How did Samuel the Nagid bridge the Jewish and Muslim cultures?

10. Discuss the way various Muslim philosophers approached the philosophy of the Greeks.

11. What are the medical contributions of Islamic society?

12. What are the characteristics of Islamic architecture?

13. Examine the extent of the trade routes for Muslim traders.

C. Western Christian civilization in the early Middle Ages

1. Trace the economic reasons contributing to the breakdown of the unity of the Roman empire.

2. When did people become aware of the break with the Roman past?

3. Why did double monasteries and convents have such appeal to the royal dynasties that supported them?

4. What were the innovations emphasized by Pope Gregory I that differed from the Eastern Christian Church?

5. Why did the Carolingians support learning? How did they do this?

6. What were the ideas in Charlemagne's letter *On the Importance of Monks Studying Classical Literature* that were reasons they should continue to study the earlier literature?

7. What were the reasons for the collapse of the Carolingian empire?

MULTIPLE CHOICE KEY

1. c
2. d
3. a
4. c
5. b
6. b
7. a
8. c
9. d
10. d
11. d
12. a
13. a
14. b
15. d

MATCHING KEY

1. c
2. g
3. h
4. d
5. a
6. b
7. j
8. i
9. e
10. f

TRUE/FALSE KEY

1. F
2. T
3. F
4. T
5. T
6. F
7. F
8. T
9. T
10. T

CHRONOLOGICAL ORDER KEY

5, 4, 1, 2, 3

CHAPTER 8

The Expansion of Europe: Economy, Society, and Politics in the High Middle Ages, 1000–1300

This chapter focuses on changes between 1000 and 1300 and the shift of power to western Europe. Economic, social and governmental changes contributed to this shift in power.

CHAPTER OUTLINE

1. The first agricultural revolution
   a. Technological advances
   b. Manorialism, serfdom, and agricultural productivity
   c. New crop rotation systems
   d. Serfdom and the limits of manorialism

2. The growth of towns and commerce
   a. Commerce
   b. Towns

3. Byzantium, Islam, and the Crusades
   a. The invasion of the Turks
   b. The First Crusade
   c. The later Crusades
   d. The consequences of the Crusades

4. Social mobility and social inequality in High Medieval Europe
   a. Nobles and knights
   b. Chivalry and courtly love

5. Politics and government
   a. Urban government

6. Feudalism and the emergence of national monarchies
   a. The problem of feudalism
   b. The Norman conquest of England
   c. Feudal monarchy in England
      i. The reign of Henry II
      ii. The reign of John and Magna Carta
   d. Feudal monarchy in France
      i. The growth of royal power in France
   e. England and France: comparisons and contrasts
   f. Germany
      i. The conflict with the Papacy
      ii. Frederick Barbarossa and Henry VI
      iii. Frederick II
   g. Iberia

7. Conclusion

IDENTIFY

1. manorialism
2. serfdom
3. three-field crop-rotation system
4. guilds
5. Kiev
6. Alexius Comnenus
7. Crusades
8. Urban II
9. Saladin
10. feudalism
11. William of Normandy
12. Exchequer
13. Thomas Becket
14. King John
15. Magna Carta
16. Edward I
17. Philip II
18. Henry IV
19. Frederick Barbarossa
20. Frederick II

MULTIPLE CHOICE

1. Which of the following accounts for increased agricultural productivity in Europe?
   a. technological innovations like the heavy-wheeled plow
   b. improved climate
   c. crop rotation
   d. all of the above

2. Craft guilds
   a. controlled prices and wages and limited competition.
   b. allowed journeymen to open shops after hours.
   c. were restricted to the cloth trade.
   d. both a and b

3. The most successful crusade was the _____.
   a. First
   b. Second
   c. Third
   d. Fourth

4. During the Fourth Crusade
   a. crusaders under the leadership of Frederick Barbarossa recaptured Jerusalem.
   b. crusaders under the leadership of Richard the Lionheart recaptured Jerusalem.
   c. the crusaders attacked Constantinople.
   d. the crusaders negotiated a settlement that allowed Christians to regain authority over the Holy Land.

5. All of the following are effects of the Crusades except
   a. a strengthening of the economic position of Genoa and Venice.
   b. the elimination of trade between the Islamic world and the West.
   c. increased animosity between the Islamic and Christian worlds.
   d. a decline in the economic and military might of the Byzantine empire.

6. Which of the following best applies to France in the year 1000?
   a. France consolidated under the Capetians and rivaled England as a military power.
   b. Feudalism had matured to allow kings to compel vassals to comply with new laws and taxes.
   c. France was actually a collection of independent territories ruled by nobles.
   d. all of the above

7. The word *feudalism* refers to
   a. the centralization of royal power through bureaucratic means.
   b. the elimination of peasant freedoms and a return to serfdom.
   c. a decentralized form of political power in which power was exercised by nobles.
   d. a form of political organization in which monarchies shared power with aristocratic assemblies.

8. At the Battle of Hastings
   a. Philip II defeated King John to claim Normandy.
   b. The duke of Normandy claimed the crown of England.
   c. King Harold valiantly fended off a Viking invasion.
   d. Christian crusaders captured Jerusalem.

9. Among the lasting achievements of the reign of Henry I was
   a. his creation of a finance bureau, the Exchequer.
   b. his use of the circuit judges to administer royal justice.
   c. his increasing reliance on Parliament as a means to raise taxes.
   d. both a and b

10. Beginning with the reign of William I, English monarchs controlled land in _____.
    a. Scotland
    b. France
    c. Ireland
    d. both b and c

11. The conflict between Henry II and Thomas Becket
    a. centered around Henry's attempt to tax the clergy.
    b. revolved around Henry's right to sentence clerics convicted of crimes in church courts.
    c. was resolved when Becket agreed to allow Henry to choose his successor at Canterbury.
    d. ultimately benefited both men.

12. Which of the following best captures the spirit of Magna Carta?
    a. Even the king must abide by the law of the land.
    b. The king reserved the right to increase taxes during a time of war.
    c. Parliament must be consulted before a monarch can raise taxes.
    d. Parliament must be consulted before a monarch can wage war.

13. The most important accomplishment of early Capetian kings was
    a. their ability to produce male heirs.
    b. their ability to extend royal authority into southern France.
    c. the speed with which they were able to subdue the French nobility.
    d. their success in battle against the German empire.

14. One result of the conflict between the German emperor and papacy was

a. the pope's right to select bishops without any interference from German emperors.

b. the selection of the emperor by the pope with veto power given to Germany's prominent nobles.

c. increased power and independence for the German nobility.

d. all of the above.

15. The end of Frederick II's reign witnessed

a. the consolidation of imperial rule over northern Italy.

b. a strengthening of the alliance between the papacy and German emperors.

c. the effective establishment of feudalism and the taming of rebellious nobles in the Holy Roman Empire.

d. the collapse of royal authority in Germany.

MATCHING

1. serfs	a. royal officials in France
2. Florence	b. recaptured Jerusalem in 1187
3. orthodoxy	c. unfree peasants
4. Basil II	d. challenged Henry IV's right to appoint bishops
5. Battle of Manzikert	e. coalition in northern Italy
6. Urban II	f. site of a Turkish victory over the Byzantine empire
7. Saladin	g. involved in the English wool trade
8. Baillis	h. the Bulgar-slayer
9. Gregory VII	i. called the First Crusade
10. Lombard League	j. correct belief

TRUE/FALSE

1. One of the benefits of the manorial system with common fields was the ability to engage in crop rotation.

2. The three-field crop-rotation system began in the Mediterranean region.

3. By 1300, the richest Europeans were merchants and bankers.

4. According to the text, all knights were considered to be nobles by the end of the thirteenth century.

5. As a code of values, chivalry distinguished knights from other members of society such as merchants and lawyers.

6. Tenth-century monarchs largely ignored the emerging towns and cities.

7. The Exchequer served as the supreme court of England.

8. By the end of King John's reign, England had lost all territory it once controlled in France.

9. Philip II was the first Capetian king to gain a significant amount of control over France.

10. The last Muslim stronghold in Spain was Granada.

PUT THE FOLLOWING ITEMS IN CHRONOLOGICAL ORDER

1. Magna Carta   _____

2. First Crusade   _____

3. Battle of Hastings   _____

4. Death of Frederick II   _____

5. Battle of Manzikert   _____

SHORT ANSWER AND ESSAYS QUESTIONS

A. Economic

1. What were the elements that brought about the agricultural revolution?

2. What impact did the first agricultural revolution have on the lives of Europeans?

3. How did food production increase?

4. What were the reasons for the commercial revolution?

5. Why were Italian cities successful in opening new trade routes?

6. What were guilds? How did they work?

B. The Crusades

1. What are the problems seen for the emperor by the author in the selection from *Advice to the Byzantine Emperor, Eleventh Century*? What can you learn about the role of the Byzantine emperor in this selection?

2. What were Urban II's reasons for calling the First Crusade?

3. What were the crusaders' reasons for going?

4. What were the (probably false) charges against the Turks in the selection from *The Spurious Letter of Alexius Comenus to Count Robert, Seeking his Aid against the Turks*?

5. What were the reasons for the success of the First Crusade?

6. What steps did Jean de Joinville take for his departure on a crusade? What were his emotions during the process?

7. Assess the impact of the Crusades on each of these areas: Byzantine empire, the Islamic world, and western Europe.

C. Social levels in High Medieval Europe

1. What made social advancement possible in High Medieval Europe? What were the new levels on the social ladder?

2. What were the requirements to become a knight?

3. What was chivalry? What were chivalric values?

D. Politics and government and feudalism

1. Explain how urban government varied by the region in which it was found.

2. Explain the importance of the personal relationship between "lord" and "vassal."

3. How was the political development in Russia connected to the Byzantine state?

4. What were the innovations in government made by Henry II in England?

5. How was Henry II's relationship with the church connected to his view of law?

6. What were the ways in which the Capetian kings of France gained royal power in France?

7. Compare and contrast the way in which monarchies in England and France centralized power. (One way to approach this is to begin by looking at the contributions of each king, then look at the final centralization.)

8. How did powerful kings come into conflict with various popes?

9. Since the selection *Frederick II Changes the Height of the Heavens* was written by a supporter of the pope, how is this used in the conflict between the church and the state?

10. What was the key to the Spanish monarchy's power?

MULTIPLE CHOICE KEY

1. d
2. a
3. a
4. c
5. b
6. c
7. c
8. b
9. d
10. b
11. b
12. a
13. a
14. c
15. d

MATCHING KEY

1. c
2. g
3. j
4. h
5. f
6. i
7. b
8. a
9. d
10. e

TRUE/FALSE KEY

1. T
2. F
3. T
4. F
5. T
6. F
7. F
8. F
9. T
10. T

CHRONOLOGICAL ORDER KEY

3, 5, 2, 1, 4

CHAPTER 9

The High Middle Ages: Religious and Intellectual Developments, 1000–1300

This chapter considers the religious and intellectual developments between 1000 and 1300. Included in this narrative is the emergence of the dominance of the papacy and its organizational effect on society.

CHAPTER OUTLINE

1. Introduction

2. The reform of the church
   a. Monastic reform
   b. Papal reform
   c. The Investiture Conflict
   d. The consolidation of papal monarchy
      i. The reign of Innocent III
      ii. Popes of the thirteenth century
   e. Decline of the papal monarchy

3. The outburst of religious vitality
   a. Christians and Cistercians
   b. The cult of the Virgin Mary
      i. Hildegard of Bingen
   c. The challenge of popular heresy
      i. Franciscans and Dominicans
   d. Jews and Christians

4. The Medieval intellectual revival
   a. The growth of schools
   b. The rise of universities
   c. The recovery of classical learning
   d. Scholasticism
      i. Peter Abelard
      ii. The triumph of scholasticism
      iii. The writings of Saint Thomas Aquinas
      iv. The pinnacle of Western medieval thought

5. The blossoming of literature, art, and music
   a. Vernacular literature
   b. Troubadour poetry and courtly romances
   c. The *Divine Comedy*
   d. Art and architecture
   e. Drama and music

6. Conclusion

IDENTIFY

1. Cluny
2. pilgrimages
3. simony
4. Pope Leo IX
5. Gregory VII
6. Concordat of Worms
7. Innocent III
8. Avignon
9. Cistercians
10. Carthusians
11. Hildegard of Bingen
12. Cathars
13. Franciscans
14. Dominicans
15. Robert Grosseteste
16. Peter Abelard
17. Thomas Aquinas
18. troubadours
19. Dante Alighieri
20. Gothic

MULTIPLE CHOICE

1. Which of the following best describes the condition of the church by the middle of the tenth century?
   a. Charlemagne's reforms finally succeeded in getting monks to follow Saint Benedict's *Rule*.
   b. The church was increasingly under lay control.
   c. Local nobles ensured that church officials maintained high moral standards.
   d. none of the above

2. The tenth-century monastic reform movement began at this Burgundian monastery:
   a. Compostela.
   b. Saint Faith.
   c. Cluny.
   d. Saint Peter.

3. The major reform of Pope Nicholas II was
   a. the outlawing of simony and promotion of clerical celibacy.
   b. preventing German emperors from nominating bishops in Italy.
   c. endowing the College of Cardinals with the authority to elect the pope.
   d. both b and c

4. Lay investiture involved
   a. a prohibition against nobles entering the clergy.
   b. a decision by Gregory VII deposing married bishops.
   c. the claim of Gregory VII to be both a temporal and spiritual leader.
   d. the appointment of church officials by non-church officials.

5. The Concordat of Worms was significant because it
   a. finally eliminated emperors from involvement in church affairs.
   b. revoked the excommunication of Henry IV.
   c. created a basis to distinguish between religious and political authority.
   d. strengthened the power of German emperors in northern Italy.

6. The most successful of all high medieval popes was _____.
   a. Innocent III
   b. Gregory VII
   c. Urban II
   d. Leo IX

7. The Cistercians
   a. followed the rule of Saint Benedict in the strictest of ways.
   b. lived in cities in order to combat heresy.
   c. established their monasteries in remote areas.
   d. both a and c

8. The Cathars and Waldensians
   a. were two new religious orders commissioned to confront the spread of heresies.
   b. were orders of university professors who challenged prevailing views.
   c. were two new religious groups that challenged Catholic orthodoxy.
   d. both a and b

9. The conflict between Pope Boniface VIII and King Philip IV was initiated over
   a. Philip's authority to tax the clergy of France.
   b. Philip's refusal to support a crusade against the Albigensians.
   c. Philip's insistence that Boniface reside in Avignon.
   d. Boniface's claim of temporal authority in France.

10. Hildegard of Bingen
    a. was an influential nun whose visions were regarded by many as inspired by God.
    b. examined subjects such as pharmacology and women's medicine in her writings.
    c. was an early feminist who called for equality for women within the Catholic Church.
    d. both a and b

11. By 1300 Christians largely regarded Jews as
    a. insignificant because of their relatively small numbers.
    b. tools of Satan who ritualistically crucified Christian children.
    c. essential to society because of their business skills.
    d. a misguided religious group who nonetheless should be extended Christian love and respect.

12. The university in Bologna gained prominence for
    a. its center for the study of law.
    b. the large number of popes who trained there.
    c. its greatest teacher, Thomas Aquinas.
    d. becoming Europe's finest institution for the study of classical art and architecture.

13. Peter Abelard
    a. attracted students throughout Europe.
    b. wrote *Sic et Non* which examined contradictory statements on one hundred fifty theological issues by church fathers.
    c. thought logic should be used to explain religious questions.
    d. all of the above

14. Robert Grosseteste and Roger Bacon both agreed that
    a. knowledge of the natural world is more reliable when based on observation.
    b. knowledge of the natural world is unattainable by humans except through divine revelation.

c. theories should be tested in laboratory settings and findings should be analyzed using mathematical principles.

d. all truth is relative and dictated by cultural patterns.

15. Saint Thomas Aquinas' writings reflect

a. his attempt to reconcile Plato's teachings with the first five books of the Old Testament.

b. his belief in the power of the human intellect and the ability of humans to affect their own salvation.

c. a willingness to analyze rationally many abstract religious questions.

d. both b and c

MATCHING

1. John XII
2. simony
3. Leo XI
4. Canossa
5. legates
6. Gratian
7. Viper Brood
8. transubstantiation
9. university
10. Goliards

a. originally meant a corporation or guild
b. codified church law
c. the miracle of the Eucharist
d. known for his decadence
e. papal officials
f. poets who lampooned the Gospels
g. began the papal reform movement
h. heirs of Frederick II
i. site of Henry IV's humiliation
j. buying and selling church offices

TRUE/FALSE

1. Fortunately for the church, most tenth-century popes were men of exemplary morals.

2. Unlike their counterparts in France and Italy, monarchs in England and Germany initiated monastic reform.

3. By the year 1000, most parish priests were married.

4. The crusade against Aragon enhanced the spiritual powers of the papacy.

5. The first crusade called for overtly political purposes was against Frederick II.

6. The greatest musical innovation of the High Middle Ages was the addition of harmonious melodies.

7. Scholastics sought to reconcile divine revelation with classical philosophy.

8. Bologna served as the model for universities throughout northern Europe.

9. Troubadour poems largely reflected an intense love for a married woman.

10. Dante's *Divine Comedy* is a masterful summation of medieval thought.

PUT THE FOLLOWING ITEMS IN CHRONOLOGICAL ORDER

1. Concordat of Worms   _____

2. Founding of Cluny   _____

3. Fourth Lateran Council   _____

4. Albigensian Crusade   _____

5. Cistercian order established _____

SHORT ANSWER AND ESSAY QUESTIONS

A. Religious

1. What were the problems that members of the monasteries were trying to eliminate and reform?

2. How did Leo IX go about reforming the papacy? Why was this necessary?

3. How does the selection *A Miracle of Saint Faith* illustrate the importance of relics and the problems that they might bring to medieval believers?

4. What was the Investiture Conflict? What was Gregory VII's goal in this conflict? Why did Henry IV oppose this?

5. How did Innocent III discipline secular rulers?

6. What were the reasons for the decline of the papal monarchy?

7. Trace the rise and fall of the papal monarchy in relationship to the secular rulers.

8. What were the two reasons that Pope Gregory VII's actions increased the religious revival and vitality?

9. In what ways was there a renewed place for women in religion during the High Middle Ages?

10. Using the selection *The Conversion of Peter Waldo*, explain how Peter Waldo displayed his religious beliefs by his behavior?

11. What did Innocent III do to strengthen the papacy in terms of the following: theology, religious organization, and the relationship to secular rulers?

B. Intellectual Developments and Literature

1. What were the four categories of major intellectual accomplishments of the High Middle Ages?

2. How did the nature of schools change? What were the reasons behind the emergence of universities?

3. What was scholasticism? How did *Sic et Non* contribute to this new approach to learning?

4. What common themes unite the literature, art, and architecture of the High Middle Ages?

5. What were the problems in the papal court addressed in the *Goliardic Parody of the Gospel of Mark, Satirizing the Papal Court* selection?

6. What are some examples of vernacular literature? Why do you think romances and narrative poems were popular? Use one as an example to show why.

7. Why is Dante's *Divine Comedy* so remarkable?

8. What changes are there between Romanesque architecture and Gothic architecture?

MULTIPLE CHOICE KEY

1. b
2. c
3. c
4. d
5. c
6. a
7. d
8. c
9. a
10. d
11. b
12. a
13. d
14. a
15. d

MATCHING KEY

1. d
2. j
3. g
4. i
5. e
6. b
7. h
8. c
9. a
10. f

TRUE/FALSE KEY

1. F
2. T
3. T
4. F
5. T
6. T
7. T
8. F
9. T
10. T

CHRONOLOGICAL ORDER KEY

2, 5, 1, 4, 3

CHAPTER 10 | The Later Middle Ages, 1300–1500

The themes of this chapter deal with the calamities of nature and the resulting economic and social dislocations. But this was also an innovative and creative period. As you read the chapter you might also consider how these two fundamental characteristics are connected.

CHAPTER OUTLINE

1. Introduction

2. Economic depression and the emergence of a New Equilibrium
   a. Climate change and agricultural failure
   b. The Black Death
   c. The impact of towns
   d. The New Equilibrium

3. Social and emotional dislocation
   a. The Jacquerie
   b. The English Peasants' Revolt
   c. Urban rebellions
   d. Aristocratic insecurities
   e. Emotional extremes

4. Trials for the church and hunger for the divine
   a. The late medieval papacy
   b. Popular piety and popular heresy
      i. Mysticism
      ii. Lollards and Hussites

5. Political crisis and recovery
   a. Italy
   b. Germany
   c. France
   d. England
   e. Spain
   f. The triumph of national monarchies

6. Kievan Rus and the rise of Muscovy
   a. The Mongol invasions

b. The rise of Muscovy
c. The rivalry with Poland
d. Moscow and Byzantium
e. The reign of Ivan the Great

7. Thought, literature, and art
   a. Theology and philosophy
   b. Vernacular literature
      i. Boccaccio
      ii. Chaucer
      iii. Christine de Pisan
   c. Sculpture and painting

8. Advances in technology

9. Conclusion

IDENTIFY

1. "Great Famine"
2. Black Death
3. The English Peasants' Revolt
4. Ciompi
5. Avignon
6. Great Schism
7. Council of Constance
8. John Wyclif
9. Hundred Years' War
10. Joan of Arc
11. Wars of the Roses
12. Ferdinand and Isabella
13. Kiev
14. Golden Horde
15. Ivan the Great
16. William of Ockham
17. Boccaccio
18. Chaucer
19. Christine de Pisan
20. Giotto

MULTIPLE CHOICE

1. Population decline in the early fourteenth century can be attributed to all of the following except
   a. the Hundred Years' War between England and France.
   b. the Great Famine from 1316–1322.
   c. an average decline in temperature.
   d. increased rainfall.

2. The Black Death manifested itself in
   a. a bloodborne illness spread only through flea bites.
   b. a bubonic and pneumonic form.
   c. a bloodborne disease spread directly by rat bites.
   d. an entirely airborne affliction spread in overcrowded towns.

3. In all probability, the Black Death spread to Europe
   a. through the Mongol invasions into eastern Europe.
   b. through Genoese ships trading in the Black Sea.
   c. by marauding armies of various Europeans.
   d. none of the above.

4. Which of the following is correct regarding the results of the plague?
   a. The population of towns and cities declined only after being struck by the plague.
   b. The plague created new economic opportunities that ultimately allowed most of Europe's cities to flourish.
   c. The plague's urban destruction was so great that Europe's urban centers would not recover until the Industrial Revolution.
   d. For two centuries following the outbreak of the plague, cities and towns had a reduced role in Europe's economy.

5. The Jacquerie in France
   a. was caused by the defeat at Agincourt and the king's effort to raise taxes.
   b. occurred when aristocrats called on French peasants to foot the bill for the ransom of Charles VII.
   c. occurred after the burning of Joan of Arc, the savior of French peasantry.
   d. none of the above

6. To distinguish themselves from merchants and financiers, artistocrats
   a. prevented all members of the middle classes from becoming ennobled.
   b. created exclusive guilds with strict membership requirements.
   c. led luxurious lives and organized chivalric orders.
   d. all of the above

7. The Great Schism refers to the period when
   a. popes rotated residences between Rome and Avignon.
   b. German emperors ruled the Catholic Church by proxy.
   c. there were two, then three popes.
   d. the College of Cardinals wrested power from the papacy and appointed a general council to lead the church.

8. Which of the following best describes the papacy at Avignon?
   a. Popes were overwhelmingly morally bankrupt and engaged primarily in secular pleasures.
   b. Popes seemed concerned mainly with bureaucratic matters and fund-raising.
   c. French kings demanded that the papacy recognize the rights of local clergy regarding church appointments.
   d. Because the popes were Italian, they retained some measure of independence from the French monarchy.

9. The Hundred Years' War broke out because
   a. English monarchs claimed the crown of France.
   b. the French navy attacked English merchant shipping in the English Channel.
   c. of English economic interests in Flanders.
   d. both a and c

10. Joan of Arc's importance to the French was her
    a. ability to rally French troops and boost morale.
    b. activities as a spy after being captured by the British.
    c. wise decision to avoid involving the weak-willed Charles VII in the war effort.
    d. both b and c

11. The Wars of the Roses refers to
    a. a rebellion by agricultural workers following the English defeat in the Hundred Years' War.
    b. the final battles of the Hundred Years' War that led to the English defeat.
    c. battles between rival aristocratic families for control of the monarchy in England.
    d. the trial proceedings that ultimately led to the burning of Joan of Arc.

12. Religious animosities between Moscow and western Europe centered around
    a. a rivalry with Catholic Poland.
    b. belief that Moscow represented the third Rome.
    c. refusal of the Catholic west to aid Byzantium against the Turks.
    d. all of the above.

13. Boccaccio's *Decameron*
    a. is an intensely religious work that fits neatly into medieval literature.

b. is a collection of secular tales of love, sex, and adventure.

c. is one of the finest examples of late medieval Latin prose.

d. both b and c

14. Technological innovations of the late medieval world include all of the following except _____.
   a. the crossbow
   b. the magnetic compass
   c. printing with moveable type
   d. the heavy cannon

15. Ferdinand and Isabella are responsible for
   a. seizing Granada, the last Muslim holdout in Spain.
   b. expelling all of Spain's Jews.
   c. writing a constitution for a new, united Spain.
   d. both a and b

MATCHING

1. Medici	a. turned Muscovy into a significant power
2. English Peasants' Revolt	b. author of *City of Ladies*
3. John Wyclif	c. naturalist painter
4. Master Eckhart	d. developed nominalism
5. Jan Hus	e. author of *Canterbury Tales*
6. Giotto	f. attacked clerical extravagance
7. Ivan III	g. led by Wat Tyler
8. William of Ockham	h. found divinity within the human soul
9. Chaucer	i. Florentine bankers
10. Christine de Pisan	j. burned at Constance

TRUE/FALSE

1. The Black Death alone was responsible for Europe's loss of two-thirds of its population between 1350 and 1450.

2. A general decline in food prices, which allowed individuals to spend more on luxury items, was a result of the Black Death.

3. The Hanseatic League was an attempt by the Holy Roman emperor to monopolize trade with northern and eastern Europe.

4. Urban rebellions in the late Middle Ages are almost always attributed to class revolts against worker exploitation.

5. The Council of Constance ended the Great Schism and thoroughly reformed the church.

6. The text suggests that discontent with the clergy stemmed from improved literacy rates among the laity.

7. The grand duchy of Kiev rose to prominence by collecting tribute for the Mongols.

8. Giotto's paintings reflect his concern for naturalism.

9. The Ciompi revolt resulted in significant, long-lasting gains for workers in the wool industry.

10. Conciliarists attempted to vest ultimate church authority in a general council rather than with the pope.

PUT THE FOLLOWING ITEMS IN CHRONOLOGICAL ORDER

1. English Peasants' Revolt _____
2. The Jacquerie _____
3. Fall of Constantinople _____
4. Death of Joan of Arc _____
5. Agincourt _____

SHORT ANSWER AND ESSAY QUESTIONS

A. Economic

1. What were the checks on agricultural expansion?

2. What were the factors that led to decreases in population?

3. What were both the short-term and long-term effects of the Black Death?

4. What were the differing causes of the Jacquerie and English Peasants' Revolt?

5. How does the description in *Froissart on the English Peasants' Revolt, 1381* portray the peasants?

6. Explain how economics contributed to urban rebellions in various places.

7. What were the reasons behind the aristocrats' insecurities during this period? How did they try to counter these perceived problems?

B. Religious reaction

1. What were the main forms of late medieval popular piety?

2. What were the advantages to the papacy of moving to Avignon? What was the problem with this move?

3. Why was increased literacy a challenge to the clergy?

4. Using the document reading *The Conciliarist Controversy,* explain why the conciliar movement was a threat to the papacy.

5. In what ways did people try to increase their religious connection to God?

6. What were the ideas of John Wyclif? Why were these a threat to the church?

C. Political

1. How was each of the major cities in Italy governed?

2. During the Hundred Years' War, how did the change of dynasty in France create difficulties for the French war effort? How did the war eventually strengthen the powers of the French monarchy?

3. Why did the English win most of the battles at the beginning of the Hundred Years' War?

4. What were the charges against Joan of Arc listed in *The Condemnation of Joan of Arc by the University of Paris, 1431*?

5. What problems were caused in England by the Hundred Years' War?

6. Why did late medieval England have political stability in spite of the turmoil of the period?

7. What were two major events that impacted Spain in 1492?

8. What four developments separated Russia from western Europe?

9. Why did the Muscovite Russians identify so closely with the Byzantines? Why did the Russians have such pronounced hostility for the West and Latin Christianity?

D. Thought, literature, and art

1. What were three characteristics of late medieval literature? Show how these characteristics can be found in the writings of Boccaccio, Chaucer, and de Pisan.

2. What are the differences between and among Boccaccio, Chaucer, and de Pisan?

3. What is the dominant trait of late medieval art?

4. What were the important innovations by Giotto in medieval art?

5. Explain how new technological advances and inventions affected people's everyday lives.

MULTIPLE CHOICE KEY

1. a
2. b
3. b
4. b
5. d
6. c
7. c
8. b
9. d
10. a
11. c
12. d
13. b
14. a
15. d

MATCHING KEY

1. i
2. g
3. f
4. h
5. j
6. c
7. a
8. d
9. e
10. b

TRUE/FALSE KEY

1. F
2. T
3. F
4. F
5. F
6. T
7. F
8. T
9. F
10. T

CHRONOLOGICAL ORDER KEY

2, 1, 5, 4, 3

CHAPTER 11 | Commerce, Conquest, and Colonization, 1300–1600

The theme in this chapter is how the economic emergence of the western part of Europe occurred. Various parts of the chapter focus on areas that preceded this or were involved in this economic expansion. Mediterranean and Atlantic economies grew and increased as well.

CHAPTER OUTLINE

1. Introduction

2. The Mongols
   a. The rise of the Mongol empire
   b. Europe, the Mongols, and the Far East

3. The rise of the Ottoman empire
   a. The conquest of Constantinople
   b. War, slavery, and social advancement
   c. Religious conflicts
   d. The Ottomans and Europe

4. Mediterranean colonialism
   a. Silver shortages and the search for African gold
   b. Mediterranean empires: Catalunya, Venice, and Genoa
   c. From the Mediterranean to the Atlantic
   d. The technology of ships and navigation
   e. Portugal, Africa, and the sea route to Asia
   f. Artillery and empire
   g. Prince Henry the Navigator
   h. Atlantic colonization and the growth of slavery

5. Europe encounters a New World
   a. The discovery of the New World
   b. The Spanish conquest of America
   c. The profits of empire in the New World

6. Conclusion

IDENTIFY

1. The Mongols
2. Chingiz Khan
3. Timur the Lame
4. Marco Polo
5. Ottoman Turks
6. Mehmet II
7. Ottoman slaves
8. Mediterranean colonialism
9. Bartholomeu Dias
10. Prince Henry the Navigator
11. Prester John
12. Christopher Columbus
13. Ferdinand Magellan
14. conquistadors
15. Price Revolution

MULTIPLE CHOICE

1. With the decline of inner-European expansion, Europe
   a. entered a period in which monarchies concentrated exclusively on domestic issues.
   b. moved east to conquer territories previously ruled by Byzantium.
   c. established sea-based colonies.
   d. embarked on a new period of internal warfare with death rates far worse than the Bubonic Plague.

2. The Mongol ruler who completed the conquest of China was _____.
   a. Chingiz Khan
   b. Qubilai Khan
   c. Timur the Lame
   d. Temujin

3. All of the following are true regarding the Mongols except
   a. they were generally intolerant of other religions.
   b. they brutally killed those who resisted their rule.
   c. they supported trade with European merchants.
   d. they spread the Bubonic Plague to Genoese during the siege at Caffa.

4. The Ottoman conquest of Constantinople
   a. prevented Europeans from acquiring eastern luxury items.
   b. was the main reason Portugal sought another sea route to Asia.
   c. had a minimal economic effect on western Europe.
   d. both a and b

5. Which of the following is not true regarding slavery in the Ottoman world?
   a. Slaves were predominant in the Ottoman army and administration.
   b. The Ottomans used Christians and Muslims as slaves.
   c. Balkan families provided slave children to pay for an imposed "child tax".
   d. Special schools trained slaves to serve the Ottomans.

6. European colonial and commercial activities in the western Mediterranean and Atlantic world reflected
   a. Europe's increased demand for African gold.
   b. the dominance of the Ottoman empire in the East.
   c. the conflict between France and Britain over control of the slave trade.
   d. both a and b

7. All of the following powers established empires in the Mediterranean except _____.
   a. Venice
   b. Sicily
   c. Genoa
   d. Catalunya

8. All of the following technological innovations benefited European sailors except _____.
   a. quadrants
   b. astrolabes
   c. marine chronometers
   d. compasses

9. Which of the following is incorrect regarding Portuguese maritime expansion?
   a. Portuguese trading posts in Africa and Asia were designed to protect against native and European attacks.
   b. Portugal became significantly involved in the African slave trade.
   c. Portuguese control of the eastern spice trade forced the Venetians to buy pepper in Lisbon.

   d. Reaching India was the initial goal for Portuguese expansion.

10. All of the following are true about Prince Henry the Navigator except:
    a. stories about his significance to Portuguese exploration appear to be exaggerated.
    b. he was a central figure in the opening of the Portuguese slave trade.
    c. his main goal was to gain control of the African gold trade.
    d. he made most of his fortune in the spice trade.

11. Native peoples used as slaves by the Spanish
    a. turned their Caribbean holdings into productive sugar plantations.
    b. helped them conquer the Aztecs and Inkas.
    c. frequently died of disease and brutal treatment.
    d. all of the above

12. The Spanish conquest of the New World
    a. led directly to a price revolution by accelerating existing inflationary patterns.
    b. required the introduction of numerous slaves to engage in sugar production.
    c. ended the silver shortage in Europe.
    d. all of the above

MATCHING

1. Temujin	a. conquered the Aztecs
2. Marco Polo	b. conquered the Inkas
3. Mehmet II	c. rounded Africa's southern tip
4. Battle of Lepanto	d. his voyage circumnavigated the globe
5. Canary Islands	e. mythical Christian king in Africa
6. rutters	f. author of *Travels*
7. Prester John	g. became Chingiz Khan
8. Bartholomeu Dias	h. silver mines in Bolivia
9. Magellan	i. Habsburg victory over the Ottomans
10. Pizarro	j. described coastal landmarks for pilots
11. Cortes	k. "jumping off point" for Columbus
12. Potosi	l. led the conquest of Constantinople

TRUE/FALSE

1. By 1600, most of the native inhabitants of the Americas had died.

2. The Ottoman conquest of Constantinople prevented Europeans from acquiring eastern luxury items.

3. Paris was the largest city in Europe by 1600.

4. After conquering Jerusalem and Cairo, Ottoman rulers assumed the title caliph.

5. The Ottomans could count on the support of Orthodox Christians in their wars against the Christian West.

6. The greatest ally of the Ottomans was Persia.

7. Venetian colonies created the processes for the production of sugar and Madeira wines.

8. Except in Iberia and Italy, slavery had disappeared from western Europe by the twelfth century.

9. The first Europeans to reach the New World were the Spanish.

10. The Spanish were not initially excited upon learning of the existence of the New World.

PUT THE FOLLOWING ITEMS IN CHRONOLOGICAL ORDER

1. Ottoman ruler assumes title of caliph   _____
2. Battle of Lepanto   _____
3. Battle of Nicopolis   _____
4. Da Gama reaches India   _____
5. Qubilai Khan conquers southern China   _____
6. Conquest of Constantinople   _____
7. Magellan's voyage   _____
8. Balboa reaches the Pacific Ocean   _____

SHORT ANSWER AND ESSAY QUESTIONS

A. Mongols

1. What impact did the Mongol conquests have on Europe?

2. Trace the expansion of the Mongol empire.

3. How did the Mongols use their economic and commercial advantages?

4. Why would *Marco Polo's Description of Java* be of interest to his readers? What do you find of interest in the selection?

B. Ottoman Turks

1. How did the Ottoman Turks benefit from the Mongol expansion?

2. How did the Ottomans increase their power?

3. Explain how the Ottomans differed from their predecessors in Constantinople in their religion and style of government. What did they see as their position in religion and its importance to the state?

4. In the reading on the *Ottoman Janissaires*, what aspect of the description reflects the writer's perspective?

5. What factors led to the successful expansion of the Ottoman empire?

C. Mediterranean colonialism

1. What were the reasons that led to the new Western orientation toward the Atlantic world?

2. What was the reason behind the change to sailing ships from oared galleys? Why was this so important?

3. What were the motives for the voyages of the Portuguese and the Spanish?

4. Explain why the Europeans were so successful in their commercial empires.

5. After reading the *Legend of Prester John* explain what the story was and why you think it had such an impact on Europeans.

6. How were the Portuguese able to control Indian Ocean trade?

D. Europe and the "New World"

1. How did colonization along the Atlantic contribute to slavery?

2. Examine the impact of the New World silver, both long and short term, on the European economy.

3. How does the selection *Enslaved Native Laborers at Potosi* help you to understand the effect of the silver market on the natives?

4. What other products, besides silver, contributed to the economic relationship between the old and new worlds?

MULTIPLE CHOICE KEY

1. c
2. b
3. a
4. c
5. b
6. a
7. b
8. c
9. d

10. d
11. c
12. d

MATCHING KEY

1. g
2. f
3. l
4. i
5. k
6. j
7. e
8. c
9. d
10. b
11. a
12. h

TRUE/FALSE KEY

1. T
2. F
3. F
4. T
5. T
6. F
7. F
8. T
9. F
10. T

CHRONOLOGICAL ORDER KEY

5, 2, 6, 4, 8, 7, 1, 3

CHAPTER 12

The Civilization of the Renaissance, c. 1350–1550

This chapter looks at the intellectual and cultural history of the period known as the "Renaissance." The term is used to describe trends in thought, literature, and the arts that emerged between 1350 and 1550.

CHAPTER OUTLINE

1. Introduction

2. The Renaissance and the Middle Ages
   a. Renaissance classicism
   b. Renaissance humanism

3. The Renaissance in Italy
   a. The origins of the Italian Renaissance
   b. The Italian Renaissance: literature and thought
   c. The emergence of textual scholarship
   d. Renaissance Neoplatonism
   e. Machiavelli
   f. The ideal of the courtier

4. The Italian Renaissance: painting, sculpture, and architecture
   a. Renaissance painting in Florence
      i. Leonardo Da Vinci
   b. The Venetian School
   c. Painting in Rome
      i. Raphael
      ii. Michelangelo
   d. Sculpture
      i. Donatello
      ii. Michelangelo
   e. Architecture

5. The waning of the Italian Renaissance

6. The Renaissance of the north
   a. Christian humanism and the northern Renaissance
      i. Desiderius Erasmus
      ii. Sir Thomas More
      iii. Ulrich von Hutten
   b. The decline of Christian humanism
   c. Literature, art, and music, in the northern Renaissance
      i. Rabelais
      ii. Architecture
      iii. Painting
      iv. Music

7. Conclusion

IDENTIFY

1. The Renaissance
2. Renaissance classicism
3. Renaissance humanism
4. Petrarch
5. Leon Battista Alberti
6. Lorenzo Valla
7. Renaissance Neoplatonism
8. Machiavelli
9. Baldassare Castiglione
10. Massacio
11. Leonardo da Vinci
12. Raphael
13. Michelangelo
14. Donatello
15. Christian humanism
16. Desiderius Erasmus
17. Thomas More
18. Ulrich von Hutten
19. François Rabelais
20. Albrecht Dürer

MULTIPLE CHOICE

1. Most scholars today regard the Renaissance as
   a. a time when Europe first became modern and a secular spirit triumphed over medieval Christian culture.
   b. a period that witnessed the rise of new monarchs who no longer felt constrained by medieval notions of rule.
   c. a term best used to describe artistic and literary trends that emerged in Italy between 1350 and 1550 before spreading to northern Europe.
   d. the rebirth of classical Roman society.

2. In comparison with the medieval world,
   a. more literary works from ancient Greece and Rome were available to Renaissance scholars.
   b. Renaissance humanists were less likely to regard ancient texts as confirming basic Christian assumptions.
   c. Renaissance culture was more worldly and secular in spirit.
   d. all of the above

3. Renaissance humanists
   a. promoted the study of logic and metaphysics as a path to understanding God's world.
   b. stressed the study of language, literature, history, and ethics.
   c. generally thought that upper-class women should gain a classical education.
   d. generally sought inward peace through rigid study of Greek in cloister-like communities.

4. The Renaissance began in Italy for all of the following reasons except
   a. the Council of Constance promoted new learning and a greater awareness of the ancient roots of Italian civilization.
   b. Italy enjoyed a significantly urbanized culture.
   c. Italy was more culturally connected to its classical past than the rest of western Europe.
   d. Italy's wealth kept scholars from seeking fortunes elsewhere in Europe.

5. Unlike civic humanists, Petrarch's notion of humanism
   a. endorsed a life of government service as the ideal human aspiration.
   b. meant solitary contemplation and withdrawal from worldly affairs.
   c. challenged Italians to unite against foreign invaders.
   d. accepted the basic tenets of scholasticism.

6. In *The Prince*, Machiavelli suggested that a ruler should be judged by
   a. his ability to unite people using Christian principles.
   b. his acceptance of republican ideals and virtues.
   c. the results of his actions.
   d. his commitment to prevailing standards of ethical and moral behavior.

7. All of the following are true of Leonardo da Vinci except
   a. he was a skilled painter, mathematician, inventor, and engineer.
   b. his paintings began the High Renaissance.
   c. his most memorable artworks treat non-Christian subjects.
   d. all of the above are true

8. Michelangelo is known for all the following except _____.
   a. *The Last Judgement*
   b. *David*
   c. *Descent from the Cross*
   d. *The Virgin of the Rocks*

9. All of the following are reasons for the decline of the Italian Renaissance except
   a. the invasion of Italy by foreign powers.
   b. the Catholic church's attempt to impose doctrinal uniformity.
   c. the decline of Italian wealth.
   d. the exodus of artists and philosophers for Paris.

10. The Inquisition dealt with Galileo by
   a. trying him for heresy and burning him at the stake.
   b. ignoring him and burning his writings.
   c. forcing him to recant his beliefs and placing him under house arrest.
   d. challenging him to debate leading Catholic astronomers.

11. A key distinction between northern Renaissance humanism and Italian Renaissance humanism was
   a. northern Renaissance humanists placed a greater value on scholasticism.
   b. northern Renaissance humanism reflected a stronger secular orientation.
   c. the writings of Italian Renaissance humanists essentially reflected the views of their patrons.
   d. none of the above.

12. Which of the following best describes the humanism of Erasmus?
   a. He intended his writings to serve as a guide for proper Christian behavior.
   b. His emphasis on Cicero made the Church restrict publication of some of his writings.
   c. He carefully sought to avoid discussion of contemporary Christian practices.
   d. both b and c

13. Thomas More's *Utopia*
    a. examined an ideal Christian community whose laws were based on the Old Testament.
    b. served as an attack on the abuses and materialism of his age.
    c. suggested that society's ills could be eliminated if peasants were given private property.
    d. called upon Christians to take up arms against the enemies of the Gospels.

14. The decline of Christian humanism coincided with
    a. the invasion of Italy by France and Spain.
    b. the pursuit of Christian humanists by the Inquisition.
    c. the rise of Protestantism.
    d. the rejection of Catholicism by most Christian humanists.

15. All of the following musical instruments were developed during the Renaissance except the _____.
    a. violin
    b. viol
    c. harpsichord
    d. piano

MATCHING

1. Petrarch
2. Alberti
3. Valla
4. Cesare Borgia
5. Castiglione
6. Botticelli
7. Charles V
8. Bruno
9. von Hutton
10. Holbein

a. painted *Birth of Venus*
b. taught how to become a "Renaissance Man"
c. painted More and Erasmus
d. burned at the stake for insisting that two worlds existed
e. endorsed the nuclear family
f. humanist and German cultural nationalist
g. Father of Renaissance humanism
h. son of Pope Alexander VI
i. proved that the Donation of Constantine was forged
j. his troops sacked Rome in 1527

TRUE/FALSE

1. It was only during the Renaissance that scholars translated the major works of Aristotle into Latin.

2. Italian aristocrats were more urbanized than most of their western European counterparts.

3. Generally, Italian Renaissance scholars were noted for their progressive ideas concerning a woman's status in society and the family.

4. Most of the great painters of the fifteenth century were from Florence.

5. Renaissance architecture disdained medieval architecture and relied exclusively on ancient patterns.

6. Among the reasons for the decline of the Italian Renaissance is the invasion of Italy by foreign powers.

7. Unlike humanists in Italy, northern Renaissance humanists worked within a university setting.

8. In *Gargantua and Pantagruel*, Rabelais satirized religious practices and superstitions.

9. Classical themes were more predominant in northern Renaissance painting than in Italian Renaissance art.

10. Opera was one of the musical innovations developed during the Renaissance.

PUT THE FOLLOWING ITEMS IN CHRONOLOGICAL ORDER

1. Publication of the Index of Forbidden Books _____
2. The sack of Rome by Charles V _____
3. Condemnation of Galileo by the Church _____
4. Charles VIII's invasion of Italy _____
5. Execution of Sir Thomas More _____

SHORT ANSWER AND ESSAY QUESTIONS

A. Humanism

1. In what new ways did Renaissance writers use classical texts?

2. What is humanism? What was the educational program of the humanists?

3. Using the readings in the text on *The Humanists' Educational Program* find examples of three different traits of humanism. What did each of these writers suggest you should study? Why do you think those subjects were chosen?

4. Why did the Renaissance begin in Italy?

5. Why were Petrarch and Valla so important?

6. What were the characteristics of civic humanism?

7. What does the selection *Some Renaissance Attitudes Toward Women* tell you about the view toward education for women during this period?

8. What are the various views on Machiavelli? Why do you need to consider both Machiavelli's *The Prince* and his *Discourses* to understand him?

9. How does the selection on *Machiavelli's Italian Patriotism* help to clarify his views?

B. Italian Renaissance Art

1. What were the three principal characteristics of Italian Renaissance art?

2. What was new about Renaissance art when compared to late medieval art?

3. Explain how each of the following artists used those characteristics in their work: Massaccio, Botticelli, Leonardo da Vinci, Bellini, Titian, Raphael, and Michelangelo. (Make sure you look at their pictures in the textbook and use them as examples as you discuss their work.)

4. What are the similarities and differences reflected in the works of artists from different cities?

5. Why was Michelangelo regarded as the supreme Renaissance artist?

6. What characteristics of the Greek aesthetic did Michelangelo use?

7. How did Renaissance sculpture differ from medieval sculpture? What similarities do you recognize with the sculpture of the Greeks?

8. Why did the Renaissance decline in Italy around 1550?

C. The Renaissance in the north

1. What was Christian humanism?

2. What are the differences between Christian humanism in the north and the earlier Italian humanism? Use Erasmus' works to illustrate these differences.

3. Use the works of two other writers from northern Europe to show the characteristics of humanism there.

4. What architectural styles were combined in the north? What were the characteristics that they adapted?

5. During the Renaissance what changes took place in the style, theory, and forms of music and its place in society?

D. General questions

1. Consider what made the Renaissance unique.

2. What were the new ways of thinking and approaching intellectual pursuits?

3. How did the view of individuals change during this period?

4. What was the new role of art in society during the Renaissance? What do you think contributed to this?

5. How did Renaissance culture differ from the culture of the High Middle Ages? How did the northern and Italian Renaissances differ from one another?

MULTIPLE CHOICE KEY

1. c
2. d
3. b
4. a
5. b
6. c
7. c
8. d
9. d
10. c
11. d
12. a
13. b
14. c
15. d

MATCHING KEY

1. g
2. e
3. i
4. h
5. b
6. a
7. j
8. d
9. f
10. c

TRUE/FALSE KEY

1. F
2. T
3. F
4. T
5. F
6. T
7. F
8. T
9. F
10. T

CHRONOLOGICAL ORDER KEY

4, 2, 5, 1, 3

CHAPTER 13 | Reformations of Religion

The focus of this chapter is on the various kinds of religious reformations that occurred during the sixteenth century. These changes in the Christian church were theological but also affected the political states.

CHAPTER OUTLINE

1. Introduction

2. The Lutheran upheaval
   a. Luther's quest for religious certainty
      i. The Reformation begins
      ii. The break with Rome
      iii. The Diet of Worms
      iv. The German princes and the Lutheran reformation

3. The spread of Protestantism
   a. The Reformation in Switzerland
      i. Ulrich Zwingli
   b. John Calvin's Reformed theology
      i. Calvinism in Geneva

4. The domestication of the Reformation, 1525–1560
   a. Protestantism and the family
      i. Protestantism and control over marriage

5. The English Reformation
   a. Henry VIII and the break with Rome
   b. Edward VI
   c. Mary Tudor and the restoration of Catholicism
   d. The Elizabethan religious settlement

6. Catholicism transformed
   a. The Catholic Reformation
      i. Saint Ignatius Loyola and the Society of Jesus
      ii. Counter-Reformation Christianity

7. Conclusion: The heritage of the Protestant Reformation

IDENTIFY

1. Martin Luther
2. Albert of Hohenzollern
3. indulgences
4. Tetzel
5. Pope Leo X
6. Diet of Worms
7. Frederick the Wise
8. Charles V
9. Ulrich Zwingli
10. Anabaptism
11. John Calvin
12. John Knox
13. Henry VIII
14. Pope Clement VII
15. Thomas Cranmer
16. Edward VI
17. Mary Tudor
18. Elizabeth I
19. Council of Trent
20. Ignatius Loyola

MULTIPLE CHOICE

1. Prior to 1513, young Martin Luther
   a. fasted, prayed, and confessed his sins regularly to gain salvation.
   b. constantly feared he would never enter heaven.
   c. painstakingly sought ways to undermine traditional Catholic teachings.
   d. both a and b

2. The late Medieval church encouraged the notion that
   a. humans could gain salvation through good works alone.

b. people could not affect their salvation in any way.

c. the concept of purgatory was a fiction that needed to be eliminated.

d. people could affect only their own lives through acts piety and charity, but not the lives of loved ones.

3. Luther developed his Ninety-five Theses in response to
   a. the election of Pope Leo X.
   b. the sale of indulgences.
   c. Albert of Hohenzollern's pluralism.
   d. the charge of heresy issued by Leo X.

4. All of the following principles form the basis of Lutheranism except
   a. justification by faith.
   b. the priesthood of all believers.
   c. the primacy of scripture.
   d. that fasting and pilgrimages reflect spiritual perfection.

5. Which of the following is not a work written by Luther?
   a. *The Praise of Folly*
   b. *To the Christian Nobility*
   c. *On Temporal Authority*
   d. *Against the Thievish, Murderous Hordes of Peasants*

6. Charles V's holdings included all of the following except _____.
   a. Spain
   b. Naples
   c. Venetia
   d. Austria

7. The continuing struggle between the papacy and conciliarists
   a. allowed several non-Italians to become pope.
   b. enabled western rulers to gain concessions from Rome.
   c. stemmed the spread of Lutheranism in southern Europe.
   d. both b and c

8. The Anabaptists left Zwingli's movement over the issue of _____.
   a. the nature of the Eucharist
   b. predestination
   c. infant baptism
   d. all of the above

9. According to John Calvin,
   a. because God has predestined some for salvation, humans can do nothing to alter their fate.
   b. pious behavior may indicate that one has been chosen for salvation.
   c. religious services should be simple and remain free of Catholic symbols and rituals.
   d. all of the above

10. The Reformation affected the practice of marriage by
    a. making it a purely religious affair without any involvement of secular authorities.
    b. strengthening parental involvement in children's choice of a marital partner.
    c. forcing people to marry at a younger age in order to produce larger families.
    d. declaring that husband and wife were equal partners in marriage.

11. Henry VIII broke with Rome because
    a. of the inspiration he received from Luther's writings.
    b. of the public's response to massive corruption in the monasteries.
    c. his first marriage failed to produce a son.
    d. all of the above

12. After the appointment of Henry VIII as Supreme Head of the Church of England,
    a. Henry organized the church along Lutheran lines.
    b. Archbishop Cranmer immediately adopted Calvinist teachings and simplified church services.
    c. the church essentially remained Catholic in doctrine and practice.
    d. the church declared a pilgrimage to Canterbury a supreme act of piety.

13. Which of the following is correct regarding the Church of England after the death of Henry VIII?
    a. Under Elizabeth the Church of England included both Protestant and Catholic beliefs and practices.
    b. Mary's war with Spain undermined Catholic authority in England.
    c. Edward VI restored Roman authority over the Church of England.
    d. The monasteries were restored despite widespread public outrage.

14. The Council of Trent
    a. refers to the internal Catholic reform movement that altered the Mass.
    b. reaffirmed traditional Catholic doctrines.
    c. accepted Protestant teachings regarding the Eucharist.
    d. is largely regarded as a triumph for the conciliar movement.

15. Saint Ignatius Loyola
    a. created the most militant Catholic organization during the Counter-Reformation.
    b. wrote *The Spiritual Exercises*, a handbook for serving God.
    c. turned the Society of Jesus into a remarkably democratic order.
    d. both a and b

MATCHING

1. Treasury of Merits	a. granted Henry VIII's annulment
2. indulgence	b. ruled by John of Leyden
3. Fuggers	c. Calvinist church
4. Tetzel	d. supervised morality in Geneva
5. Zwingli	e. storehouse of good deeds
6. Geneva	f. forgiveness of penitential obligations
7. Münster	
8. Reformed Church	g. sold indulgences for salvation
	h. Catholic order for women
9. Presbyterians	i. Calvinists in Scotland
10. Consistory	j. German banking family
11. Cranmer	k. organized his religious reforms in Zurich
12. Ursilines	
	l. ruled by John Calvin

TRUE/FALSE

1. German peasants saw in Luther's ideas an opportunity for liberation from feudal obligations.

2. Luther upset his father by becoming a Dominican friar.

3. At the Diet of Worms, Luther was declared an outlaw although the decree was never enforced.

4. The German nobility regarded Lutheranism as an opportunity to overthrow the existing social order.

5. Mennonite communities are one of the legacies of Anabaptism.

6. Calvinism was a much more aggressive form of Protestantism than Lutheranism.

7. John Knox "reformed" the church in Scotland.

8. Protestantism differed from Catholicism by approving the sanctity of marital sexuality.

9. Most of the works placed on the Index of Prohibited Books were political and scientific treatises that challenged Catholic "science."

10. The Council of Trent eliminated the selling of indulgences.

PUT THE FOLLOWING ITEMS IN CHRONOLOGICAL ORDER

1. Opening of the Council of Trent   _____
2. Posting of the Ninety-five Theses   _____
3. John Calvin gains control of Geneva   _____
4. Death of Ulrich Zwingli   _____
5. The Diet of Worms   _____

SHORT ANSWER AND ESSAY QUESTIONS

A. The importance of Martin Luther

1. Explain the meaning and importance of Luther's "tower experience."

2. What is Luther's view of the "justice of God"? How does this differ from the medieval church's view?

3. How did Luther's view regarding salvation also differ from the medieval church?

4. What were the implications of Luther's criticism of the abuses of the church? Why was this different from other critics of the same period?

5. What were the reasons behind the charges against Luther by Pope Leo X?

6. Explain the three primary theological premises of Luther.

7. What were the reasons for such dissatisfaction with popes, particularly in Germany?

B. Political implications within Germany

1. What problems did Emperor Charles V face in his ability to rule within Germany?

2. How were political rulers able to control or limit religion within their own states?

3. Why did various German princes support Luther's religious practices within their own territories?

C. The spread of Protestantism

1. Why did Switzerland emerge as an important center for sixteenth-century Protestantism?

2. Compare and contrast the theological views of Zwingli and Luther.

3. Explain the role of John of Leyden in the changes in the Anabaptists' interpretation of religious practice. How was this interpretation also applied to the state?

4. In his *Institutes of the Christian Religion*, what did Calvin use as the starting point to his theological interpretation?

5. Explain the differences between Luther and Calvin regarding church government.

6. How and why did Geneva become the center for spreading the Reformed religion?

7. How did the notions of family and marriage change during the Reformation? In what ways did this also involve

the political state? Why did parents feel they should choose marriage partners for their children? Include examples from the selection *Luther on Celibacy and Women* to illustrate your view.

D. The English Reformation

1. Why did England become a Protestant country?

2. What were Henry VIII's motives for wanting to break his marriage bonds?

3. What problems faced Clement VII in his consideration of Henry VIII's annulment?

4. How did the break between the English church and the church at Rome occur? What were the political components involved in this break?

5. What are the basic tenets of the Church of England's theology as found in *The Six Articles*?

6. Explain how the theology kept changing in England depending on which of Henry VIII's children were on the throne. What was the final settlement?

F. Catholicism transformed

1. What were the differences between the "Catholic Reformation" and the "Counter-Reformation"?

2. What were the results of the Council of Trent regarding theology or doctrine and the role of both the clergy and the laity? What other changes were a result of decisions made?

3. Examine the growth of the Society of Jesus from its beginning to becoming the "shock troops" of the Counter-Reformation. What were the original goals and the ensuing activities? How do these reflect qualities found in the selection *Obedience as a Jesuit Hallmark*?

4. What were the results, both religious and political, of the Counter-Reformation?

G. Reformation influences

1. What were the influences of the Renaissance on the reformations of belief? What are the major differences between Reformation values and Renaissance values?

2. Examine the influence of the political world on the reformations.

MULTIPLE CHOICE KEY

1. d
2. a
3. b
4. d
5. a
6. c
7. b
8. c
9. d
10. b
11. c
12. c
13. a
14. b
15. d

MATCHING KEY

1. e
2. f
3. j
4. g
5. k
6. l
7. b
8. c
9. i
10. d
11. a
12. h

TRUE/FALSE KEY

1. T
2. T
3. T
4. F
5. T
6. T
7. T
8. T
9. F
10. F

CHRONOLOGICAL ORDER KEY

2, 5, 4, 3, 1

CHAPTER 14 | Religious Wars and State Building, 1540–1660

One theme of this chapter is the connection between religion and political authority. There is also a focus on the reasons that the period between 1540 and 1660 is considered one of the most turbulent in European history. The resulting doubt and uncertainty produced a quest for political understanding and new approaches to literature and art.

CHAPTER OUTLINE

1. Introduction

2. Economic, religious, and political tests
   a. The price revolution
   b. Religious conflicts
   c. Political instability

3. A century of religious wars
   a. The German wars of religion to 1555
   b. The French wars of religion
   c. The revolt of the Netherlands
   d. England and the defeat of the Spanish Armada
   e. The Thirty Years' War

4. Divergent paths: Spain, France, and England, 1600–1660
   a. The decline of Spain
   b. The growing power of France
      i. Cardinal Richelieu
      ii. The Fronde
   c. The English civil war
      i. The origins of the English civil war
      ii. Civil war and Commonwealth
      iii. The restoration of the monarchy

5. The problem of doubt and the quest for certainty
   a. Witchcraft accusations and the power of the state
   b. The search for authority

6. Literature and the arts
   a. Miguel de Cervantes (1547–1616)
   b. Elizabethan and Jacobean drama
   c. Mannerism
   d. Baroque art and architecture
   e. Dutch painting in the "golden age"

7. Conclusion

IDENTIFY

1. Price Revolution
2. Charles V
3. Peace of Augsburg
4. Huguenots
5. Catherine de' Medici
6. Henry of Navarre
7. Philip II
8. Spanish Armada
9. Elizabeth I
10. Thirty Years' War
11. Petition of Right
12. Cardinal Richelieu
13. Charles I
14. Oliver Cromwell
15. Gianlorenzo Bernini
16. Diego Velázquez
17. Thomas Hobbes
18. William Shakespeare
19. John Milton
20. Mannerism

MULTIPLE CHOICE

1. All of the following contributed to the Price Revolution except the
   a. increasing demand for food.
   b. influx of bullion from Spanish America.
   c. increasing supply of food produced.
   d. rising population of Europe.

2. According to the Peace of Augsburg
   a. Charles V reestablished religious unity in the Holy Roman empire.
   b. Charles V divided his holdings among his sons.
   c. within the Holy Roman empire, the ruler of a territory determined the religion of the territory.
   d. Lutheranism was officially recognized as a heresy.

3. The Saint Bartholomew's Day massacre refers to the event after
   a. Catherine de' Medici decided to rule France in her name.
   b. leading Huguenots assembled in Paris for a wedding between Henry of Navarre and Catherine de' Medici's daughter.
   c. King Henry III of France died with no male heirs, thus opening a battle for control of the crown.
   d. Huguenots went on a rampage to start a civil war.

4. The Edict of Nantes
   a. allowed Huguenots to worship freely throughout France.
   b. ended the religious rivalries in France and allowed Henry of Navarre to become king.
   c. limited the rights of Catholics to worship in regions with a Calvinist majority.
   d. granted limited religious freedoms and political rights to French Protestants.

5. Philip II assembled the Spanish Armada
   a. to convince Queen Elizabeth to take his hand in marriage.
   b. because of England's support for the Dutch rebels.
   c. because the Dutch opened the dikes, forcing the Duke of Alva to transport troops by water.
   d. initially to thwart the threat of English pirates to Spanish shipping.

6. France entered the Thirty Years' War
   a. to support the reestablishment of Catholicism throughout the Holy Roman empire.
   b. to test their forces against the mighty Swedish army under Gustavus Adolphus.
   c. to prevent Habsburg forces from winning.
   d. to deal a final death blow to Calvinism in France.

7. The Peace of Westphalia
   a. reflected the growing power of Austrian Habsburgs.
   b. allowed Spain to retake the Netherlands over the protests of France.
   c. turned the Holy Roman empire into a unified military power.
   d. began a period when France emerged as the dominant power on the continent.

8. Spain's greatest problems in the seventeenth century were _____.
   a. economic
   b. political
   c. social
   d. none of the above

9. Cardinal Richelieu's policies served to
   a. strengthen the power of the monarchy.
   b. promote greater religious toleration.
   c. strengthen France economically through overseas conquests.
   d. unite France and Britain against the decaying Spanish empire.

10. English Puritans
    a. resented any attempt to alter the Church of England.
    b. supported efforts to restore some Catholic practices.
    c. wanted Calvinism to triumph in England.
    d. supported the monarchy in the English civil war.

11. The Petition of Right included all of the following except
    a. a declaration that all taxes not approved by Parliament were illegal.
    b. a new definition of treason.
    c. a prohibition against arbitrary imprisonment.
    d. a prohibition against quartering soldiers in private homes.

12. Oliver Cromwell's rule in England is best described as _____.
    a. an enlightened republic
    b. a puritanical dictatorship
    c. a parliamentary form of government
    d. a religious democracy

13. King Charles II of England
    a. restored bishops to the Church of England.
    b. agreed to rule with Parliament.
    c. recognized the validity of the Petition of Right.
    d. all of the above

14. All of the following are true concerning witchcraft except
    a. accused witches in Protestant countries were almost always treated leniently.
    b. many believed that witches had made a pact with the devil.
    c. authorities employed torture to secure confessions.
    d. witchcraft trials reflected the growing power of the state to protect society.

15. Jean Bodin would have most likely argued that
    a. sovereignty must be vested in an all-powerful monarch.
    b. representative government is essential for protecting citizens' rights.
    c. rulers who became tyrants should be overthrown.
    d. none of the above

MATCHING

1. Huguenots	a. author of *Leviathan*
2. Catherine de' Medici	b. Charles II's army in the English civil war
3. Duke of Alva	c. instituted the Council of Blood
4. Gustavus Adolphus	d. author of *Don Quixote*
5. Duke of Sully	e. French Calvinists
6. The Fronde	f. began as a revolt against Mazarin's policies
7. Cavaliers	g. the "Lion of the North"
8. Roundheads	h. Queen of France
9. Hobbes	i. promoted agricultural and manufacturing improvements in France
10. Cervantes	j. parliamentary forces in the English civil war

TRUE/FALSE

1. The spread of Calvinism within France benefited from the conversion of several female aristocrats.
2. During the Thirty Years' War, France supported the Catholic forces.
3. The English civil war began after Charles I attempted to have several parliamentary leaders arrested.
4. William Shakespeare was more popular than Christopher Marlowe in Elizabethan England.
5. Michel de Montaigne's *Essays* reflect his pervasive skepticism of the benefits of religious toleration.
6. Gianlorenzo Bernini and Peter Brueghel were masters of Mannerism.
7. William of Orange was a diehard Catholic who supported Philip II's attempts to suppress Calvinism in the Netherlands.
8. During the "Protectorate," Cromwell flooded the House of Lords with Puritans.
9. Baroque architecture often was designed to promote Catholic principles.
10. Thomas Hobbes' writings reflect his profoundly pessimistic views of human nature.

PUT THE FOLLOWING ITEMS IN CHRONOLOGICAL ORDER

1. Peace of Westphalia _____
2. Saint Bartholomew's Day Massacre _____
3. Spanish Armada _____
4. Beheading of Charles I _____
5. Beginning of Stuart Dynasty _____

SHORT ANSWER AND ESSAY QUESTIONS

A. Economic

1. Explain what brought about soaring prices and the effect of this inflation on society.
2. How did the Price Revolution place new pressures on governments?

B. Religious conflicts

1. What were the basic issues of the German wars of religion that began in 1555? How were these issues resolved?
2. What were the various reasons the French wars of religion continued for so long?
3. What were the stipulations and guarantees in the Edict of Nantes? How did this change France?
4. Compare the attitudes of Charles V and Philip II in relation to the Netherlands.
5. What were the various reasons for the political rebellion in the Netherlands?
6. What were the various causes behind the conflict between England and Spain?
7. What were the issues in the Thirty Years' War? Why did it shift from a "religious" civil war to one of international politics?
8. In the selection on *The Destructiveness of the Thirty Years' War,* what were the various kinds of cruelty and destructiveness?

C. Divergent paths: Spain, France, and England, 1600–1660

1. Why was Spain's economy its greatest weakness? What contributed to this economic decline?
2. Explain how the French state was strengthened and centralized by Henry IV and then Richelieu.
3. Read the document *Cardinal Richelieu on the Common People of France* and then put into your own words what he thought of them.

4. What were the problems James I faced as king of England? How did he attempt to deal with these?

5. Explain how Charles I contributed to his problems as king of England.

6. Compare the views toward the political consequences of the two selections in *Democracy and the English Civil War*. What does each have to say about the role of government?

7. How was religion relevant in the English civil war?

D. Doubt and certainty

1. Why was there a "desperate search for new foundations upon which to reconstruct some measure of certainty"?

2. Show how witchcraft was linked to both the belief system and the political state. Go back to the reading from *Simplicissimus* in the previous chapter and see if you can find how it illustrates the acceptance of witchcraft as a reality.

3. What are the basic premises of Montaigne? How are these reflected in the document *Montaigne on Skepticism and Faith?*

4. According to Bodin, what is the reason a political state exists? What did he regard as the best kind of government?

5. What were the differences between Bodin and Hobbes in their views of government?

6. How did Pascal try to appeal to both intelligence and emotion to convince people of the truth of Christianity?

E. Literature and the arts

1. What are the different facets of human nature represented in the characters in *Don Quixote*?

2. How did Christopher Marlowe and Ben Jonson display human nature?

3. Discuss how Shakespeare's plays illustrate a variety of characteristics of human nature. How did his emphasis change over time?

4. What are the characteristics of the two schools of "Mannerism"?

5. What set El Greco's art apart from that of his contemporaries?

6. What made Dutch painting unique? How could this be seen in its themes? How did this also deal with human nature?

7. Compare and contrast Rubens and Rembrandt in their approach to painting.

8. Using specific artists' paintings, consider how art is a reaction to wars and bloodshed.

MULTIPLE CHOICE KEY

1. c
2. c
3. b
4. d
5. b
6. c
7. d
8. a
9. a
10. c
11. b
12. b
13. d
14. a
15. a

MATCHING KEY

1. e
2. h
3. c
4. g
5. i
6. f
7. b
8. j
9. a
10. d

TRUE/FALSE KEY

1. T
2. F
3. T
4. F
5. F
6. F
7. F
8. F
9. T
10. T

CHRONOLOGICAL ORDER KEY

2, 3, 5, 1, 4

CHAPTER 15 | Absolutism and Empire, 1660–1789

This chapter deals with notions of sovereignty. The dominant kind of sovereignty during this period was absolutism. The chapter explains how it was brought about and how it worked. It explains how the idea of absolutism was linked to empire and the growth of empires. Various other kinds of governments that were alternatives to absolutism are also examined. The chapter also deals with the political theory bchind various kinds of government. Finally, the last part of the chapter looks at how government, economics, and colonies were connected in the late seventeenth and early eighteenth centuries.

CHAPTER OUTLINE

1. Introduction

2. The appeal and justification of absolutism

3. Alternatives to absolutism
   a. Limited monarchy: The case of England
      i. The reign of Charles II
      ii. King James II
      iii. The Glorious Revolution
      iv. John Locke and the contract theory of government

4. The absolutism of Louis XIV
   a. Performing royalty at Versailles
   b. Administration and centralization
   c. Louis XIV's religious policies
   d. Colbert and royal finance
   e. The wars of Louis XIV to 1697
   f. The War of the Spanish Succession
   g. The Treaty of Utrecht

5. The remaking of central and eastern Europe
   a. The Habsburg empire
   b. The Rise of Brandenburg-Prussia
   c. Autocracy in Russia
      i. The early years of Peter's reign
      ii. The transformation of the tsarist state
      iii. Peter's foreign policy
      iv. Catherine the Great and the partition of Poland
   d. Commerce and consumption
      i. Economic growth in the eighteenth century
      ii. A world of goods

6. Colonization and trade in the seventeenth century
   a. Spanish colonialism
   b. English colonialism
   c. French colonialism
   d. Dutch colonialism
   e. Contrasting patterns of colonial settlement
   f. Colonial rivalries

7. Colonialism and empire
   a. The "triangular" trade in sugar and spices
   b. The commercial rivalry between Britain and France
   c. War and empire in the eighteenth century world
   d. The American Revolution

8. Conclusion

IDENTIFY

1. absolutism
2. Louis XIV
3. Charles II
4. James II
5. The Glorious Revolution

6. John Locke
7. Versailles
8. Jean Baptiste Colbert
9. William of Orange
10. War of the Spanish Succession
11. The Treaty of Utrecht
12. Frederick William, "The Great Elector"
13. Frederick William I
14. Peter I
15. Table of Ranks
16. Catherine the Great
17. Emelyan Pugachev
18. joint-stock company
19. "triangular" trade
20. Treaty of Paris

MULTIPLE CHOICE

1. The theory of absolutism
   a. gave rulers complete sovereignty in matters of law, justice, and taxation.
   b. allowed great, hereditary nobles, working through representative bodies, to limit the authority of kings to tax land.
   c. claimed to be as divinely inspired as a father's absolute authority over his family.
   d. both a and c

2. By 1700, all of the following regions were ruled by absolute monarchs except _____.
   a. Russia
   b. Prussia
   c. England
   d. France

3. One of the ways Louis XIV managed to curtail the power of the nobility was by
   a. exiling his great nobles to French colonies in the Americas.
   b. forcing his great nobles to reside at Versailles for part of the year.
   c. enlisting them as his spies and primary police force.
   d. all of the above.

4. American colonists protested taxes imposed after the Seven Years' War because they
   a. were levied without the colonists' consent.
   b. bankrupted the colonies.
   c. were collected by British soldiers who harassed and bullied colonists.
   d. all of the above.

5. The Glorious Revolution had its origins in
   a. a desire by Parliament to restore Catholicism.
   b. an attempt by England's leading barons to subvert Parliament.
   c. the fear that a Catholic dynasty would eliminate Protestantism.
   d. both b and c

6. The English gained all of the following rights as a result of the Glorious Revolution except
   a. *habeas corpus*.
   b. trial by jury.
   c. the right to petition the monarch through Parliament.
   d. the right to worship freely and hold public office regardless of one's religion.

7. According to John Locke
   a. absolutism was the best guide to restore order and create prosperity.
   b. government was designed to protect life, liberty, and property.
   c. government should redistribute property to the landless to avoid social revolution.
   d. citizens had no right to overthrow absolute monarchs.

8. The League of Augsburg
   a. sought to preserve a balance of power in Europe.
   b. was an attempt to crush the spread of Catholicism in England.
   c. settled the issue regarding a Spanish successor to Charles II through wise diplomacy.
   d. allowed the Habsburgs to extend their authority over the United Provinces.

9. The Treaty of Utrecht allowed for all of the following except
   a. Austrian control of part of northern Italy.
   b. Spanish control over the slave trade.
   c. British control over Gibraltar and several former French colonies in the New World.
   d. Spain to remain a colonial power in the New World.

10. The nobility under Frederick the Great Elector
    a. was allowed to enserf peasants.
    b. served as the officer corps of his army.
    c. saw their taxes increase dramatically.
    d. both a and b

11. Peter the Great's policies of "westernization" were essentially aimed at
    a. increasing agricultural productivity through enserfment of the peasants.
    b. enhancing the prestige of the Russian orthodox church by introducing new bishoprics.
    c. increasing Russian military power.
    d. turning Russia into the most elegant and culturally refined great power in Europe.

12. Significant economic developments in the eighteenth century included
    a. the growth of urban manufacturing.
    b. the introduction of new crops and methods of farming.
    c. the increasing use of rural labor in textile production.
    d. all of the above.

13. The most profitable commodity (commodities) imported into England from its colonies in the New World and Asia was/were _____.
    a. tobacco
    b. slaves
    c. potatoes
    d. sugar

14. In comparison to French and Spanish colonists, English colonists
    a. relied exclusively on agriculture for survival and trade.
    b. rarely married natives.
    c. neglected the customs and practices of their homeland to create a unique culture.
    d. quickly abandoned initial coastal settlements to build plantations in the heartland of North America.

15. The "triangular" trade primarily involved the trans-Atlantic shipping and sale of _____.
    a. fish and furs
    b. sugar and slaves
    c. cotton, sugar, and tobacco
    d. both a and b

MATCHING

1. House of Orange
2. Charles II
3. John Locke
4. Louis XIV
5. Quietists
6. Jansenists
7. Jean Baptiste Colbert
8. Habsburgs
9. Frederick William I
10. *Streltsy*
11. Duma
12. Emelyan Pugachev

a. practiced personal mysticism
b. wrote *Two Treatises of Government*
c. Russian national assembly
d. Dutch rulers
e. rebel Cossack leader
f. elite palace guard in Russia
g. "that known enemy of chastity and virginity"
h. "the sergeant king"
i. Louis XIV's finance minister
j. strictly adhered to the doctrine of predestination
k. the "Sun King"
l. rulers of Austria, Hungary, and Bohemia

TRUE/FALSE

1. One of the appeals of absolutism was its promise to restore order and stability after years of turmoil.

2. In Protestant countries, Protestant churches maintained a considerable degree of independence under absolute monarchs.

3. By the 1670s, Charles II patterned his reign after the absolutism of Louis XIV.

4. The 1689 Act of Toleration finally allowed Catholics to worship freely and to hold public office.

5. The Glorious Revolution formally united England and Scotland.

6. Louis XIV relied on the upper middle class to serve in his bureaucracy.

7. Unlike other absolute monarchs, Louis XIV promoted religious toleration to strengthen his hold on France.

8. With the weakening of Ottoman power, Brandenburg-Prussia became Austria's main rival in central Europe.

9. Peter the Great's Potsdam Giants were instrumental in defeating the revolt of the *streltsy*.

10. Joint-stock companies allowed investors to determine managerial decisions.

11. The goal of Peter the Great's foreign policy was to gain warm water ports for his navy.

12. Catherine the Great is regarded as an enlightened monarch because of the extensive social reforms she enacted during her reign.

13. By the beginning of the nineteenth century, Poland had disappeared from the map of Europe.

14. French Protestants who fled to Prussia helped Berlin establish a silk-weaving industry.

15. Early English North American colonists made significant strides in converting American Indians to Protestantism.

PUT THE FOLLOWING ITEMS IN CHRONOLOGICAL ORDER

1. Peace of Nystad _____
2. Treaty of Utrecht _____
3. Ottoman siege of Vienna _____
4. Glorious Revolution _____
5. Founding of Jamestown _____
6. Treaty of Paris _____

SHORT ANSWER AND ESSAY QUESTIONS

A. The appeal and justification of absolutism

1. What were the aims of absolutist rulers?

2. Why was absolutism accepted? What were the advantages of it and what were the disadvantages?

3. What was necessary for absolutism to work?

4. What problems did rulers encounter in becoming absolute? In what ways did they overcome these?

5. Compare the two selections in *Absolutism and Patriarchy.* How do Bossuet and Filmer each support absolutism? How do they differ in their reasons for their support?

B. Alternatives to absolutism

1. What were various styles of government? Which were alternatives to absolutism?

2. What made the English style of government unique? How did this come about?

3. Compare the reigns of Charles II and James II in England.

4. Describe the events of the Glorious Revolution. What changes occurred in the English government as a result?

5. Discuss John Locke's theory of government. Explain his concept of how government originated and developed and its resulting form. How does Locke's theory differ from absolutism?

6. What is meant by the contract theory of government?

C. Absolutism and Louis XIV

1. How did Louis XIV strengthen his control over France?

2. How did Louis XIV bring the nobles under control and reduce their power?

3. How were the *intendants* beneficial to Louis XIV's government in terms of power and finances?

4. What are the reasons Louis XIV thought it necessary to control religion? Explain how he accomplished this goal.

5. Explain how Jean Baptiste Colbert's economic policy strengthened Louis XIV's absolutism. Why are these policies a good example of mercantilism?

6. In the selection *Mercantilism and War,* how does Colbert illustrate how mercantilism supports Louis XIV's policies of war?

7. Compare and contrast the wars of Louis XIV in terms of their objectives, opponents, and outcomes. Did the wars' long-term results accomplish Louis's goals?

8. What were the stipulations of the Treaty of Utrecht? What was its impact on the balance of power between and among European states?

D. Remaking of central and eastern Europe

1. What changes were behind the growing power of Prussia?

2. What were the problems and limitations the Habsburg emperors had in trying to centralize their power?

3. What were the contributions of each of the Prussian rulers (Frederick William, Frederick I and Frederick William I) in building an absolutist state?

4. Compare and contrast absolutism in Prussia with that in France under Louis XIV.

5. How did Peter the Great make Russia into a great European power?

6. How did Russian absolutism differ from the other European states at the time?

7. How did Peter the Great bring the nobility under his control? How did he try to "westernize" the nobility?

8. What were Peter the Great's successes in foreign policy? How did Catherine add to the territories of Russia? In what directions did this expansion occur?

9. What were the reasons behind the partition of Poland?

E. Economic

1. What contributed to population growth in the countryside?

2. What contributed to population growth in the cities?

3. How did developments in trade and manufacturing contribute to the rising prosperity of northwest Europe?

4. What changes in manufacturing also occurred in the countryside?

5. Describe the emerging consumer goods market.

F. Colonization and trade

1. How did English colonists try to gain profits? How did this differ from the efforts of the French and Spanish?

2. What new products came from the various colonies that belonged to the European powers?

3. How were joint-stock companies organized? What was innovative about these organizations?

4. What was the model of colonization of the French and Spanish? How did the English model differ? What were the reasons for these differences?

5. What differed in the work forces in the various colonies? How did this affect social interaction between the levels of society?

G. Colonialism and empire

1. What was "triangular" trade? What did traders at each of the three points gain? Give an example of how it worked using two colonial powers.

2. How valuable was colonial commerce to the European states?

3. In colonial trade, what was the link between the European governments and the merchants? How did this lead to advantages for the British over the French?

4. Explain how the British and French competition in colonial efforts involved various conflicts of war.

H. The American Revolution

1. How did the British government treat complaints of their colonists in North America?

2. What were the reasons behind British colonial policies?

MULTIPLE CHOICE KEY

1. a
2. c
3. b
4. a
5. c
6. d
7. b
8. a
9. b
10. d
11. c
12. d
13. d
14. b
15. b

MATCHING KEY

1. d
2. g
3. b
4. k
5. a
6. j
7. i
8. l
9. h
10. f
11. c
12. e

TRUE/FALSE KEY

1. T
2. F
3. T
4. F
5. F
6. T
7. F
8. T
9. F
10. F
11. T
12. F
13. T
14. T
15. F

CHRONOLOGICAL ORDER KEY

5, 3, 4, 2, 1, 6